"Michael York is as engaging a writer as he is a brilliant actor. His memoir works on several levels — as travel writing and as an insight into the process of a profoundly committed actor.

Making a film is always an adventure and an education and with this book, Michael York shares both with his audience. Lest this sound too serious, it's surprisingly funny as is Michael York."

WILLIAM FRIEDKIN

"Once again Michael York takes us on a journey with him, and whew, the places he's been!"

WHOOPI GOLDBERG

"In *Dispatches from Armageddon,* Michael York has turned out one of the most readable, literate, and insightful works ever written on the process of making movies. It may have started out as a personal diary, but his dispatches ended up as richly revealing, often riveting overview of the motion picture process. York's extraordinary understanding — both on a creative and a human level — add a dimension that filmgoers will find fascinating . . . and filmmakers absolutely essential to understanding their craft. His insights literally change the filmgoing process for the avid filmgoer. York also makes it clear that if he had not chosen acting as a profession, he would have made one hell of a writer."

**RICHARD BROWN, PROFESSOR OF HUMANITIES,
NEW YORK UNIVERSITY**

"It's such fun to be with the Devil at Armageddon! — especially when the Devil is the life-loving Michael York, who takes us on an intimate and fascinating journey into the making of a movie while reminding us that 'the Devil' is not confined to the movies. Entertaining and thought-provoking, York's tale proves again that the Devil has all the best tunes — and that one way to keep the Devil away is to affirm life with the spirit of appreciation that shines out from this book."

**PROFESSOR BETTY SUE FLOWERS,
UNIVERSITY OF TEXAS, AUSTIN**

DISPATCHES FROM ARMAGEDDON

Making the Movie *Megiddo*
. . . a Devilish Diary!

For Jane

with very best wishes

Published by
Smith and Kraus, Inc.
177 Lyme Road, Hanover, NH 03755
www.SmithKraus.com

Cover and Text Design by Freedom Hill Design, Reading, Vermont
Front cover photo by Frank Ockenfels, Los Angeles, CA, December 2000.
Back cover artwork by P.O.V. Design, North Hollywood, California

First edition: December 2001
9 8 7 6 5 4 3 2 1

Library of Congress Cataloging In Publication Information
York, Michael.
Dispatches from Armageddon : Making the movie Megiddo. . . a devilish
diary! / Michael York. —1st ed.
p. cm.
ISBN 1-57525-311-9
1. York, Michael. 2. Megiddo, Omega Code 2 (Motion picture) 3. Motion
picture actors and actresses — Great Britain — Biography. I. Title.
PN2598.Y68D57 2001   791.43'028'092
QBI01-701091

DISPATCHES FROM ARMAGEDDON

Making the Movie

MEGIDDO

...a Devilish Diary!

Michael York

A SMITH AND KRAUS BOOK

For Pat,
who shares the Journey,
with much love.

CONTENTS

Write the things which thou hast seen, and the things that are, and the things which shall be hereafter.

REVELATION I, 19

He lies like an eyewitness.

RUSSIAN PROVERB

CHAPTER ONE

The Combat Zone

The Omega Code was a kind of modern miracle. It was a movie that came from the Wilderness and ended up on the Mount. Made for a mere $7.2 million by a company with modest credentials in film production and without much conventional advertising, it succeeded in attracting a vast audience and turning itself into the biggest limited release film of that apocalyptic year, 2000. The *USA Today* newspaper trumpeted that it was "the hit Hollywood overlooked" with, as another journal breathlessly put it, "eye-popping numbers."

My involvement began in early February 1999 when I was sent the script, then entitled *The Code*. Although the exact significance of much of its religious content eluded me, there was something very compelling about this story centered around a dynamic media mogul, Stone Alexander, the role on offer to me. Misusing his global influence to gain world domination, Stone is thwarted by powers of goodness both human and divine.

In more specific, Christian terms, it represented the delineation of the prophecy that "In the last days a world leader will rise up and make peace in the Middle East, rebuild Solomon's temple and usher in a period of world peace under a new Roman empire. Then, possessed by Satan, he will declare himself God and embark on a reign of terror until the Lord comes and destroys him."

For Stone Alexander was also the Antichrist in this updated version of the prophecy — not surprisingly, an intriguing and showy role. It validated the old saying that "the Devil has the best tunes" and underlined the problem that John Milton had with his *Paradise Lost* in which Satan constantly hogs the limelight.

As an actor, I have always operated as much from instinct as from advice. After that initial trinity of queries — where? who with? how much? — I usually defy logic, obeying only that buzz in the pit of the guts that signifies approval. I have always preferred to be proactive rather than play it safe— at all times bearing in mind that surprisingly truthful Hollywood mantra: "Nobody knows *anything.*"

The script by Stephan Blinn was complex and ambitious, firing in a great many different directions. Its main story, highlighting the apocalyptic showdown between good and evil, was cross-referenced with the Bible Code theory, positing that within the good book are secret, divinely encrypted messages that can be accessed by a mathematical formula. Sir Isaac Newton apparently spent the last years of his life trying unsuccessfully to crack this cipher that, as an introductory statement on the finished film put it, "is said to contain the whole of human history."

I had recently read a fascinating book about this code that, among a myriad of other instances, predicted the birth of Hitler and the death of Princess Diana. Such a grand theme was not easily dismissed, and I decided to pursue it further. Accordingly, the producers, Matthew Crouch and Lawrence Mortoff, and the director Robert Marcarelli, came to my Los Angeles home for a meeting on the evening of February 3rd, 1999.

Matthew, or Matt as he was familiarly known, though slightly built, seemed to fill the room with his energy, eloquence, and enthusiasm. He was the son of Paul and Jan Crouch, who owned the Trinity Broadcasting Network, America's largest religious broadcasting system. This "Church Electric" reached seventy million households on four hundred TV stations and five thousand cable systems, and it was also beamed by satellites from space — a setup that Stone Alexander would no doubt have coveted. Paul Crouch was executive producer of the movie, which was being made for his TBN Films.

Larry Mortoff, lean, sharp and funny, was a veteran producer, a duty also shared by the director, Rob Marcarelli, who had a background of making religiously themed family films. Later, all three would remind me wryly of my initial declaration that the script was either "totally meretricious or totally meritorious."

Matt, who seemed to have inherited all of his parents' evangelical fervor, was quick to persuade me of the latter interpretation. Perhaps realizing that, for many, Christian entertainment was a contradiction in terms, he assuaged my reluctance to act in what might be perceived to be a religious tract, however well intentioned.

He explained that he wanted to enlarge the scope of TBN's work and play Hollywood at its own game, making a film geared to modern cinematic sensibilities that would appeal to both the faithful and to fans of fast-paced thrillers. In this way he would be preaching to the converted as well as to the uninitiated. He claimed that there was a vast constituency of potential cinemagoers who stayed away because they disliked the dubious fare being provided — the "Californication," as it has been called — where gratuitous sex and violence masqueraded as entertainment.

Rob told me of the plans to shoot on location in the two great millennial cities of Rome and Jerusalem, rejecting the financially tempting, but limiting, option of filming in some studio — or even in a dressed-up corner of TBN's Orange County headquarters. An invitation to travel was a strong inducement for both myself and my wife, Pat, who had once been a travel editor for *Glamour* magazine and who was now a wide-ranging, freelance photographer with recent exhibitions of her work as far afield as New York and St. Petersburg. As another saint, Augustine, so eloquently put it: "The world is a book, and those who do not travel read only one page."

I tried to suppress this response and listen objectively to all three enthusing about the film's special effects to be created by Vision-Arts, the Los Angeles company that had provided the wizardry for *Godzilla* and *Independence Day.* One of these ambitious effects was the recreation of Jerusalem's Dome of the Rock shrine, which was to be blown up on camera and, in fulfillment of prophecy, restored by Stone Alexander.

After they had left, I thought long and hard about this Alexander character. He certainly provided a charismatic "arc" to play, beginning as a wealthy philanthropic media tycoon — from the same mold as Rupert Murdoch and Ted Turner — who unites the world and solves so many of its problems that he is appointed its first Chancellor. Using the arcane knowledge and power supplied by the Bible Code, he eventually develops into a psychopathic monster: from "an Angel of Light" to "the Beast" of the Book of Revelation.

It was the very religious source of the story that presented the most interesting challenge. As the philosopher Søren Kierkegaard noticed, our culture tends to sidestep confrontation with the spiritual, so that we are "tranquilized by the trivial." And it was a number-crunching scientist, Albert Einstein, who insisted that "the most beautiful thing we can experience is the mysterious. It is the source of all true art and science." As for my own spiritual leanings, they have an affinity with that student of comparative religion in Shaw's *Major Barbara* who declares, "and the problem is, I believe every one of them." I also acknowledge the truth of the assertion that "Talent is your gift from God; what you do with it is your gift to God."

The only reservation I had was a practical one. I was still recovering from some hip surgery — the result of so much energetic swashbuckling in my cinematic youth — and was still walking with a cane. However, I awoke the next morning with a certainty that I should accept this intriguing invitation to flesh out and inhabit such a fascinating role.

It reminded me of when I had played for the other side of the religious equation; Franco Zeffirelli had asked me to incarnate John the Baptist in his monumental *Jesus of Nazareth* film in 1976. John had presented similar challenges to those I now faced with Alexander: how to create a charismatic character of almost mythic proportions and yet one whose fundamentally human dimensions were equally evident. With both roles, legions of believers stood ready to be betrayed; the risks were numerous — what better reason to accept?

I signed on along with my co-stars, Casper Van Dien and Catherine Oxenberg. Casper was a rising young actor who had made a stir in *Starship Troopers* alongside Michael Ironside, who was also aboard our film. Dr. Gillen Lane was an interesting stretch for Casper, enabling him to use all of his energetic charm to play a motivational guru, recruited by Alexander to further his nefarious goals. Lane discovers the truth, both literally and spiritually, and, in a tense finale, thwarts his employer's monstrous plans.

Catherine, with her aristocratic European genes and popular appeal, was a good choice for Cassandra, Alexander's seductive amanuensis. Stone would have admired the despotic ways of her namesake ancestor, Catherine the Great. The script hinted at a sexual connection in the relationship, one that I thought worth making overt during subsequent filming. Cassandra certainly used her feminine wiles to ensnare Lane into Stone's malevolent trap.

As it happened, Catherine and Casper were falling in love in real life at the time, which gave their scenes a certain verisimilitude and resonance. They certainly looked wonderful together in their shared happiness. The degree of Casper's devotion was indicated by this former Tarzan's willingness to abandon his carnivorous past and adopt Catherine's meatless regimen. They both developed an unerring instinct for finding vegetarian restaurants in the most improbable places.

Michael Ironside was Dominick, Stone's priestly shadow, and was as tough as his name. I had worked with him before and admired his brooding intelligence and raw power. Also prominent and pervasive throughout the film were the two End-Time prophets predicted by the Book of Revelation. If budgetary restraints prevented them from speaking in the specified "tongues of fire," they certainly illuminated the screen with their fiery rhetoric.

We began with a "table reading" of the script, a practice standard in the theater and television, but unusual in the cinema, where often one's first stab at a characterization was in the very first shot on the first day of filming. It was useful, too, in breaking the social ice. I was introduced to our leading players including Casper who, despite a tiring journey from London the day before, was vibrant with energy and ideas. It was also helpful to actually hear how the dialogue sounded. Stephan Blinn, our writer, tousled of hair, boyish of mien, was on hand to defend or emend. Occasionally, real problems with speech or structure were revealed, and it was so much easier to fix them at this stage rather than later on the set where pressures and passions were more intense.

We assembled at Rob Marcarelli's home, a Malibu house

that even sported its own modest cliff-hugging vineyard. It was perhaps Rob who encouraged the characterization of Alexander as a similar wine lover, owning vines that produced "the finest Barolo in the land." Adding one's own personal touch to a role's patina of personality was a welcome exercise. For my part, I played up Alexander's passion for Shakespeare, adding to the few quotes already there, a practice subsequently taken even further in the *Megiddo* script.

Getting the words right was one thing; getting the look right was equally vital. Our costume designer produced some interesting twists on contemporary "power" dressing. High-collared, tie-less shirts were worn with conservative suits as well as flamboyant velvet jackets. My robes for the re-dedication of the Temple in Jerusalem were a subtle cross between the sacerdotal and the secular.

Filming began on the 22nd of February in a hangar at the Santa Monica Airport inside a company jet — appropriate symbolism for a project now poised to take off on a strange and detour-filled excursion that was as much predictable as it was unknown. It was there I met for the first time Paul Crouch, who turned out to be as handsome and engaging a man as he was on television. I was pleased to note that, in confirmation of Stone Alexander's "power" wardrobe, he was wearing an elegant, collar-less shirt too. He instantly interviewed me for his TBN, and, as it turned out, the entire progress of the filming would be similarly reported from the set. "Two thousand years ago, Jesus told his followers vivid stories and parables about life," Paul Crouch explained, "today we use film and television."

My real screen baptism came a few days later. As is so often the case, a scene that occurs at the end of the film was shot first. I always welcome this disruption of the natural linear order as it requires one to really think about character and anticipate its development. The scene depicted Stone's self-proclaimed "coronation" on Jerusalem's Temple Mount where he declares that he has become "both God and King." There was no question of easing one's way into the role; this required a heady plunge in the deep end, right into the middle of an intense, fast-paced scene that demanded both grandiloquence and plausibility.

We filmed in a modern synagogue in the Simi Valley near Los Angeles and, going instantly into creative overdrive,

Michael Ironside and I enjoyed inventing elements of the ceremony: I even made him kiss my ring! At times I felt inspired in the exact sense of the word, feeling myself to be a conduit for some strange force. Perhaps this was merely the result of fatigue, for we filmed all night using a congregation largely made up of volunteers whose patience and enthusiasm were positively saintly. I wondered at what point in our long day's journey into night they became aware that filming was not the glamourous business that was fabricated in the media, but something more akin to sweated labor.

Our next location was in the real Jerusalem. Pat and I travelled there via London, with a brief opportunity to see family and friends, agents and that quintessential London activity, theater. I even managed to catch a rehearsal of *Cabaret* put on, not without controversy as to its suitability, by my nephew Henry's school in Lewes. The Nazi theme was extended by seeing David Edgar's play *Speer* in London that night with Klaus Maria Brandauer playing the title role of Hitler's right-hand man — a position that for many, would put him in the same league as the demonic Alexander.

I had worked in Israel many times since my first visit

in the early 1960s, when I played Romeo with a student group from Oxford University. Like Romeo with his Juliet, I was instantly smitten with this land where history seemed fresh-forged daily. In Jerusalem we performed in the theater where Adolf Eichmann had been recently tried for his supporting role in that supreme star-crossed tragedy, the Holocaust. I was there again making a film when another devilish protagonist, Saddam Hussein, was also enacting his "Mother of All Wars." Most recently and peaceably, I was back to record a live broadcast of the *Magnificat* from Jerusalem. One sensed the power in the very fabric of this ancient city, dense with prayers and faith, the witness to so much hope and violence.

There were reunions now with some crew of that Gulf War–era film of ten years before and also with Oded Teomi who had acted in it with Liv Ullmann and myself. He was now playing the Israeli Prime Minister who, at first resisting Alexander's maneuvering in Arab-Israeli affairs, is mollified by Stone's procurement of a peace treaty between the two ancient foes.

We filmed this scene on the Mount of Olives, with a

chilly wind animating the proceedings. The old city spread below us, a soft sun illuminating its ochre stones and glinting off the Dome of the Rock on the Temple Mount. This most contentiously prized part of a disputed city would be destroyed and rebuilt thanks to Alexander's self-promoting philanthropy — and our special effects team. For, in fulfillment of another key prophecy, "He who controls Jerusalem in the Last Days will control the world."

We travelled out of the city and up to Masada, and then down to the Dead Sea for a bath in its thick salt water that banished all remaining traces of jet lag. Israel has always had an invigorating influence, and I found I could now blithely throw away the cane I still used for walking. We drove to the Galilee where my character, as Antichrist, had witnessed his Nazarene nemesis nurture a faith that had changed the world. Passing through the newly accessible city of Jericho, Pat photographed Israeli and Palestinian soldiers sitting comradely together, as if symbolizing the reality of Alexander's peacemaking breakthrough.

On the return journey, something made me take a detour to Megiddo. Little did I suspect that this place would provide a key location and, indeed, the title of the sequel to *The Omega Code*. Commanding a strategic position over the Jezreel valley, its name means "Place of Battles, Place of Triumphs," and like Jerusalem whose approaches it controls, it has been prized and disputed since time immemorial. The Pharaohs were here fighting the Israelites, as were the British against the Turks in the First World War, their victorious commander even styling himself with a self-aggrandizing panache worthy of Stone Alexander: "Allenby of Megiddo."

After a week of filming in Israel, we headed back over the Mediterranean to the city that had once been its conqueror: Rome. I had first come here in the mid-1950s, before the postwar recovery and boom had put a confident smile back on the nation's strained economic face, ushering in *la dolce vita* and swarms of Vespa scooters and noisy little Fiats. Now we were headquartered at the Grand Hotel Plaza, a dignified old dowager of an hostelry that lived up to her imposing name.

The modern world had intruded little on her old-fashioned confines; one sensed that the telephone had but recently replaced the bellpull, and the television set seemed as inappropriate as a Damien Hirst sculpture in the Vatican. Our high-ceilinged suite extended onto a huge balcony overlooking the crowded Via del Corso below, which seemed to still echo with the ghostly hoofbeats of Roman charioteers racing down its straight and narrow course.

Rome itself was playing hard to get, hiding its charms behind a veil of scaffolding and netting as, in homage more to Christo than to Christ, its monuments and treasures were being cleaned for the forthcoming millennial celebrations. Our arrival coincided with the first official day of *Primavera,* and the first green of fresh foliage coaxed by a warming sun complemented the capital's dusty pigments and washed ochres. Pat and I wandered around what had once been the center of the world, delighting in unexpected alleys and piazzas, fountains and footpaths, reliving previous visits and discoveries. I praised my good fortune that I was a pain-free walker again.

Encountering Rob and Stephan in the Piazza Navona, we continued our impromptu tour together, discovering new delights as well as new insights into our film, for discussion of the script was endless. This was continued over pasta at Passetto's, where, during a similar long, leisurely lunch, Pat had once photographed Frederico Fellini and his longtime collaborator, the composer Nino Rota. (It was the 1960s and Fellini politely enquired if Pat, fresh from "swinging London," was wearing her night dress!) Rota had composed the score of my very first film, *The Taming of the Shrew,* directed by Franco Zeffirelli; I keenly recall a subsequent occasion in Rome when he sat down at Franco's drawing room piano and spellbound us with his haunting theme for *Romeo and Juliet.*

We joined the Sunday throng in St. Peter's Square and were even blessed by the Pope from his distant balcony. He might have withheld such bounty had he known the Antichrist was in his audience! Fascinated by the surrounding outpouring of devotion, I imagined Stone Alexander on the same balcony, preaching his seductive, malevolent gospel to the same adoring upturned faces as he had done so recently on the Temple Mount.

The next day I was punished for such hubristic thoughts when filming resumed in an apocalyptic rainstorm that drowned our attempts to stage a garden party scene in a small, bosky park on the Aventino hill. Damp extras huddled for shelter while we counted out the wasted hours with coffee spoons and teacups in our trailers. As gray daylight was fading, we salvaged one scene from this frustrating washout where Stone reviews a flyby of his warplanes, the light of madness in his megalomaniac eyes being the chief illumination.

We returned to successfully retake the same scene two days later in more appropriate bright sunshine. At the "wrap" everyone drove north to our next location, Bracciano, perched on the slopes of the round volcanic lake of the same name. The little, huddled town was dominated by the battlemented Orsini-Odescalchi castle that served both as headquarters for our film unit and as Stone Alexander's European base.

The hulking fortress seemed to permanently imprison the winter. In the fickle spring weather, it was hard to keep warm and, on occasion, even harder to operate basic vocal mechanisms. Lubricating hot drinks became a necessity, rather than a luxury, as huge burners belched hellfires of flame a few ineffectual feet into the chilly fastness. There was still snow on the distant Apennines, making a shot of Alexander and Lane listed in the script as "in Switzerland" totally plausible.

All this reminded me of filming John the Baptist for Zeffirelli. I had been chained up in the dungeon of a similar wintry, stony fortress in Monastir in Tunisia wearing just a hair shirt and a rapt expression, while all around the crew shivered in layers of clothing more appropriate to skiing than scripture. The castle interiors, though, were exquisitely decorated and it was a thrill to work amid such antique beauty.

In contrast, we stayed in the modern Hotel Alfredo down on the lakeshore. Its slightly barrack-like atmosphere was offset by the beauty of the views from its balconies, by the generous cuisine served in its more traditional water's-edge trattoria, and by the charm of the youthful staff.

There was one spectacularly beautiful young woman serving breakfast who Pat — then photographing an endearing series of people going about their daily business, but in the nude — almost persuaded to pose for her. Losing her nerve at the last moment, this Bracciano Venus meekly returned to the mundane world of cornflakes and cappuccino, leaving us all disappointed.

On the 27th of March, my birthday and our thirty-first wedding anniversary, we awoke to a huge, vivid double rainbow that encircled and lit up the lake. Later that evening, in a cozy restaurant crammed within a cluster of old buildings in town, we celebrated with a cake provided by Casper, Catherine, and her enchanting daughter, India. It was a family affair: Matt's beautiful Madonna-esque wife, Laurie, was there with their two sons, Caylan and Cody, as well as Matt's brother, Paul Jr., the director of photography in the second unit. We raised our glasses in salutation. It seemed a most propitious way in which to start my new year, playing a major role in an ambitious movie in one of my favorite countries, surrounded by such congenial company.

Production in LA was resumed at the old, abandoned City of Angels hospital, where we filmed the scenes of Alexander's astonishing resuscitation after being shot in the head. Matt's office was here, located in its former bomb shelter. (As our film had scenes where Alexander threatens the world with nuclear war, this seemed both entirely appropriate and somewhat ironic.) Hospitals are uninviting places at the best of times, but this run-down building was especially unattractive. It presented a sharp contrast to the last hospital I had been in — the Hadassah in Jerusalem — where Pat had photographed doctors and operations while I admired the exquisite Chagall windows.

The old Park Plaza Hotel, whose handsome high-ceilinged ballroom made a plausible match with the Bracciano's authentically antique interiors, was our final location. It had now been transformed with high-tech computer screens and grandiose desks into Alexander's office. In his typical, ruthless way, Stone Alexander had by this time taken over and, in a role reversal that I welcome in every film, was now playing me. It was fun to follow his outrageous dictates, and to share in the creation of this seductive, multilingual monster. Improvisation was by now relatively easy, and even unavoidable at times when the organically expanding character hit against the confines of now outdated and irrelevant dialogue. It was as if someone else were speaking through me, a sensation as welcome as it was strange.

We completed the movie on April 17th, working all night on the final scene where Alexander is overwhelmed by the forces of good. This crucial shot was "in the can" just as, in a kind of sympathy, the dawn filtered into the room, similarly banishing the darkness with its life-affirming rays.

I took off my costume and makeup with the usual mixture of relief and regret experienced at the end of every film. There had been only thirty-five shooting days — a phenomenally short time for a project with multiple locations and effects, filming in three countries on two continents. For a time, at least, Stone Alexander was no longer going to rule my life.

The next I heard of this exasperating, exhilarating character was when some footage was assembled for promotion at the Cannes Film Festival. "This is a story that could not have been told until now, until the end of the millennium," Matt Crouch proclaimed in the accompanying publicity material, "because only now have current events and modern technology been able to shed so much new light on so many ancient discoveries."

The entire film was now in the process of being pieced

together by a master editor, Peter Zinner. An Oscar-winner for *The Deer Hunter,* he had also been singled out for his work on the *Godfather* saga, and he was thus eminently qualified to handle epic themes — or, as the Cannes material put it, to "combine Hitchcockian plot twists and psychological horror to weave a tale of international terror and intrigue."

A subsequent face-to-face encounter with this supreme international terrorist, Stone Alexander, came in late August in a LA studio, at a "post-synch" or, to give it its grandiose title, an "Additional Dialogue Replacement" session. Here speech could be re-recorded to match lip movements on screen, a particularly useful tool for clarifying dialogue that was indistinct or had become inaccurate. Words and phrases could be changed if necessary — "yes" even mutating to "no" if lip movement allowed — and the whole tempo and tenor of a performance adjusted to match the rhythm and pitch of the almost completed film.

As our sound recordist was both experienced and proficient, there was relatively little to do. The chief pleasure (and occasional torment) lay in seeing the film cut together for the first time — all those little moments so painstakingly gathered now seamlessly integrated into free-flowing sequences.

The word on the film, now called *The Omega Code,* was optimistic, and I learned that more money was being spent on making the special effects even more special. Further cuts and changes were then made after several test previews, a now standard practice in an industry that constantly tries to second-guess its public's moviegoing tastes. It has to be said, though, that the public tries equally hard to second-guess its entertainers: Cinema is one of the few enterprises where the public pays *before* knowing what it is purchasing. But at least the preview system allows the public a certain participation in the multi-viewpointed system in which movies are collaboratively created.

On October 7th I was invited to a screening of the finished film. Maintaining objectivity on such an occasion is always difficult. One tends to concentrate on one's own performance and to be constantly bombarded with extraneous considerations of which a normal viewer would be unaware — such as why certain sequences were moved or removed, whether haircuts matched, and what music was used, and when. A film constitutes a visual diary, each frame being a record of that charged and vivid time. *I Am a Camera,* indeed, and I remember my reaction at seeing *Cabaret* for the first time at a press screening, and my entirely opposite reaction at its premiere the next day, when despair metamorphosed into delight.

This time I was equally impressed with what I saw. The film seemed to have cost twice its actual budget, and I particularly admired its relentless pace. "The end has begun," the final frame cryptically declared, commenting both on the film's theme and on that other revelation — the enormous task that now lay ahead to promote it. However, it was with a sense of huge relief and much incipient excitement that I left the dark screening room for the bright, less apocalyptic world outside.

Would the great, fickle, unpredictable public like it too? Early information about ticket sales was encouraging. Phil Zacharetti of Regal Cinemas reported that, "Other than *Phantom Menace* we have not had a film sell that many advance tickets."

All further speculation was put to rest when, on October 13th, 1999, with a simultaneous presentation in Houston, the film was given its premiere at the Bruin Theater in Los Angeles' Westwood neighborhood, near the UCLA campus. There was a palpable sense of occasion: Kleig lights lit up the sky, press cameras flashed and crowds of onlookers, like well rehearsed extras, thronged and applauded the Chosen walking the red carpet to the spectacle.

Along the way, from a raised floodlit platform, Matt and Laurie Crouch were televising the event worldwide for TBN in a nonstop sequence of commentary and interviews. It was here that Matt proved to be his father's son, preaching the word with a bright-eyed, evangelical fervor that stared down any last vestige of incipient cynicism or disbelief.

The results were spectacular; some would even detect a divine influence. Opening in only 305 theaters, many of them sold out, *The Omega Code* accumulated the best dollars-per-screen take of any of the competing top ten films. Like a David overcoming Goliath, it trounced such mega-hyped and expensive studio fare as *The Fight Club* that brawled its way onto thousands of screens. Matt later ruefully confessed that the only reason the movie opened in so few theaters was that, "We only had enough money for 305 prints." And in an act of pure faith and commitment, much of that money had been obtained by mortgaging his family's house!

Instead of burning out quickly, the film burst into a firestorm of favor. The *USA Today* newspaper reported that, "People are calling and clicking for *The Omega Code,* the Christian apocalypse movie that opened two weeks ago and is expanding to more theaters. Executives at MovieFone and its Internet branch, MovieLink, say *Omega* is showing the biggest response of any film since the early days of *The Blair Witch Project.* The movie is one of the five most-asked-for films in Dallas, Cleveland, Miami and Las Vegas. In Los Angeles it has moved in and out of the No. 1 position." As the Box Office Guru web site observed, vindicating Matt's original intention: "They're almost beating the studios at their own game."

This extraordinary response occurred despite the film's "Parental Guidance" rating, earned not by the film's satanic content, but by the presence in it of another iconic image of glamour and destruction, the gun. "We do blow things up and there are guns," Michael Harpster, the marketing chief of the film's distributor, Providence Entertainment, admitted, adding in an understatement, "We're dealing with the end of time, so clearly, that would be a fairly violent event."

Much of the success was attributable to the movie's extensive promotion on TBN, but Matt had also encouraged a response among fellow churchgoers by organizing a group of 2000 volunteers, his "Prayer Warriors," who ensured that it almost became an act of faith to attend the film and bear witness. One especially zealous recruit even proselytized to tattoo parlors, strip joints, saloons, and other dens of conventional iniquity.

In keeping with our technological times, the word was also spread from that other worldwide pulpit: the Internet. Our film took a cue from *The Blair Witch Project*, another "niche" movie that had built a fanatical audience online. "Call it *The Blair God Project*," *Time* magazine enthused, "made on a modest budget. . . the quality of its writing, acting and production is remarkably high."

Matt Crouch called me one day to report that there had been twelve million hits on *The Omega Code* web site, amounting to some 12,000 a day. There were 500,000 alone on the film's opening weekend. Its poster had been downloaded some 200,000 times and the film's chat room was the most in demand of any comparable site. He also confided that one of the most enthusiastic reviews had been given to him by a young boy at the premiere: "This is the best Christian horror flick I've ever seen!"

All this unconventional advertising was important, as it helped to compensate for the meagerness of the film's promotional budget. In today's marketplace, where it costs as much to sell a film as to make it, this was an essential consideration. Such turning of cinematic water into fine wine prompted *USA Today* to observe that "The phenomenal grass roots success of the surprise hit, *The Omega Code,* has swept the nation in a wave of *Omega*-mania." It was left to the *New York Times* to muse elegantly on "A sleeper movie awakened by a hungry audience." The buzz started to reach many of my friends who, frustrated by the lack of advertising, began calling me to find out where they, too, could see the film.

It was perhaps the Internet that helped spread word of

the film's success abroad. Under the banner heading, "God's Big Break" and the equally irreverent byline, "Why The Devil Is Doing Great Box Office," London's *Guardian* newspaper printed a full page report, while the tabloid *Express* summed it all up with uncharacteristic restraint and truthfulness: "*The Omega Code's* success has stunned the film world."

At one point I was invited to the CNN studios to try and account for this phenomenon. I surmised that perhaps the film played to a certain paranoia that was now rapidly building as the millennium approached. Certainly the timing seemed fortuitous, a factor confirmed by Hal Lindsey, the author of another apocalyptic chiller, *The Late, Great Planet Earth*. "*The Omega Code* has a most important message," he declared, "It couldn't have come out at a better time."

The actual millennium passed and still the film continued to create a stir, having now palpably left its niche and crossed over to a wider public. A video version appeared, and it sold in impressive numbers. Wal-Mart, the American superstore, increased its order from an initial 50,000 to an astonishing 250,000 units. Even the US Government caught the excitement and, perhaps in acknowledgment of the threat posed by Alexander's deadly war games, ordered some 50,000 videos as a cautionary tale for troops worldwide.

In all, some 1.3 million units were shipped, making it, astoundingly, the third most popular title after that other special effects–driven morality drama, *Star Wars — The Phantom Menace* that, coincidentally, was being produced by Pat's son, Rick McCallum. It also appeared encoded on DVDs to boost these lofty figures. By July the film had earned $12.5 million, making it the premier limited-release film of the year. In confirmation of these "boffo" numbers, the film trade bible, *Variety*, listed it in the 125th position in its roll call of the year's top 250 films. All this seemed to validate the film's own publicity claim that *The Omega Code* was not just a movie, but a miracle.

Back in September 1999, before the film's fortune had been determined, the *Los Angeles Times* reported that Paul Crouch had entertained a long-held cinematic dream to make a film based on Armageddon. "My dad would like to do a picture that has a $20 to $30 million special effects budget," Matt was reported as saying, "It's based on Revelation and is an apocalyptic kind of thing."

Talk of a sequel was now definitely in the air.

CHAPTER TWO

Mobilization

The new millennium began without much detectable sign of apocalyptic mayhem — except perhaps in France. I had been invited there to head the jury of a film festival at Gerardmer in the Vosges mountains. Pat and I took the TGV train from Paris and sped by an endless vista of devastation. Like one of the plagues from *The Omega Code,* a rare and unseasonable hurricane had levelled almost every other tree en route, reducing the landscape to the kind of grim no-man's-land captured in photos of World War I battlefields. Why the French had been singled out for tribulation remained obscure, but it marked the beginning of a spate of unusual and belligerent weather worldwide. Certainly war would be a key element of my ensuing year. Fortunately, this destruction did nothing to diminish our appreciation of the festival's delectable combination of good food and movies, made only slightly less enjoyable by their being relished in the hellish confines of impenetrably smoky rooms.

Back in Los Angeles, I met up with Matt Crouch and, in a puritanically smoke-free room, discussed the reality and logistics of an *Omega Code* sequel. The premise of the new story was to be another quotation from the Book of Revelation, Chapter 17, Verse 8: "The Beast shall ascend out of the bottomless pit, and they that dwell on earth shall wonder when they behold the Beast that was, and is not, and yet is."

Stephan Blinn had written a potential scenario, "both a sequel and a prequel," that picked up at the exact moment where the previous film finished, with Stone Alexander overwhelmed by the forces of light. "A head slams into frame, smashing down on the hardwood floor," his outline began. "Blood pours from a massive re-opened head wound. Cold, unblinking eyes stare straight ahead. Camera creeps closer as the pupils dilate. Closer. We push inside his eyes and are zapped into a dizzying vortex of fleeting memories and unsettling visions until Stone pops awake, now a young man deposited by his father at various military academies across Europe."

Stephan continued, blowing his trumpet as vigorously as an ancient Israelite his ram's horn as he warmed to his theme: "A unique and riveting blend of intense drama, psychological horror and mind-blowing science fiction that aims at taking the audience on a roller-coaster ride through the living hell that is the Great Tribulation as Stone Alexander, the Antichrist, uses his power to coerce the world to gather its armies at the plains of Megiddo for what will be the Final Battle of all mankind."

I had to put the script down and take a deep breath before continuing. I read on with mounting interest about Stone's childhood and the crucial relationship with his father whom he will later kill. I learned of his education and the forces that shaped his dark purpose. These included his indoctrination by a sinister Rasputin-like figure who serves as the predicted False Prophet and helps Stone to clone himself. The resulting monstrous, surreal, Golem figure will validate Stone's claims for Godhead.

Finally, the culminating battle of Armageddon is fought at Megiddo. The Antichrist is defeated and returned to the everlasting fires where "We pull back out through a pair of eyes to find ourselves back in Stone's office and his dead eyes staring blankly at us." Phew!

This was an enormously ambitious scenario — again, one that had elements that would appeal to those of the faith, as well as enough bravura special effects to drop the jaw of the average moviegoer seeking some epic excitement. How literal these effects would be remained, literally, to be seen, but my first impressions were more than positive: That pit-of-the-stomach buzz was there again.

Matt and I discussed the initial plans for the shoot, scheduled for eight weeks in July or August. We would again return to Israel and Bracciano. This time the budget was bigger: the $4 million allotted for special effects alone represented over half the cost of the previous film.

At this time I was finishing a book that I had co-authored

with my best friend of forty years, Adrian Brine. *A Shakespearean Actor Prepares* was set for publication in May, and to clear my schedule for a summer shoot meant accelerating the proofing process. Soon my head fairly reverberated with verbiage from the Bard and I suggested playing up Stone's own predilection for Shakespearean quotations — perhaps highlighting the darker works, and even the infamous, unnameable "Scottish" play with its similar investigation of the plausibility of evil in human form. Indeed there was an *Omega* paradigm in Macbeth's "And oftentimes, to win us to our harm,/ The instruments of Darkness tell us truths,/ Win us with honest trifles, to betray's/ In deepest consequence."

By mid-March, around the time *The Omega Code* video was so successfully launched, my deal had been settled and a start date for the film, now entitled *The Battle at Megiddo*, was set for July 16th. I had also been invited to serve as a producer, a role I relished as much as playing Stone Alexander, and I hoped I could bring to it a small measure of the latter's overbearing self-confidence and ambition.

The only possible complication was that I was also

scheduled to start another ambitious film in May. *One Life Later* was an epic story of a man's spiritual awakening and redemption, to be filmed in England, India, France, and Arizona, and directed by the veteran cinematographer, Jack Cardiff. This presented a head-on conflict of Megiddan dimensions; but I had learned by now to trust "the Divinity that shapes our ends" that has a habit of arranging our rough-hewn timetables to the benefit of everyone if it was meant to be.

Meanwhile, I continued work on the book and also — something that engaged me with increasing frequency and pleasure — lectured around the country. I spoke on Shakespeare in a chilly Richmond and a frozen Port Huron, and on "Wagner and Shakespeare" in a rain-swept Los Angeles. Wagner's epic stories of gods and monsters, of catastrophe and redemption, provided an appropriate leitmotif to my ongoing meditations on *Megiddo*.

As is common in Hollywood where perfection of the script before filming is a cardinal and laudable aim, a new writer, John Fasano, was hired to polish the text and provide a fresh objectivity. On April 5th, I joined him and my fellow producers, Matt, Larry Mortoff, and Gary Bettman, to brainstorm on his revised version.

John was a big, bluff, bearded figure — a genial cross between a Hell's Angel and a junior Sumo wrestler — with an equally generous wit. He immediately endeared himself by proclaiming his fondness for D'Artagnan and my *Musketeer* films that had enlivened both our youths. John had come up with some interesting new ideas. In the bottom-line shorthand employed to pitch films to executives who had no time to listen, let alone read, he summarized his concept as "*Patton* Meets *The Omen*." He introduced the idea of a sibling Cain and Abel rivalry between Stone and a younger brother, David, one that would eventually place them on opposing sides in the great final conflict.

The story's entry and exit through Alexander's dead eye was cut, as was the cloned Golem figure, even though cloning and its sinister potential were daily in the news. The False Prophet, now called Raistlin, was redefined, and the romantic rivalry between Stone and David over the daughter of the head of the military academy was more sharply triangulated. There were scenes of international intrigue from Washington to Beijing and even one in Israel's Knesset.

Again, my concern was that the film's depiction of the fulfillment of biblical prophecy should be made vital, organic, and interesting not only to an audience of believers, but to the general public as well. I felt that ensuring this in subsequent script revisions could be the most useful way in which I, as someone outside the TBN family, could wear my producer's hat.

In early May, Larry Mortoff called to ask me to reprise Stone Alexander in a short promotional trailer for *Megiddo,* to be shown at the upcoming Cannes Film Festival. He had recently been with Matt in Kenya, filming some extraordinary scenes of a crowd of a million devotees at an open-air religious meeting at the University of Nairobi.

Matt had managed to persuade the participants to "act" out several key reactions, such as applauding, kneeling, and running away in panic. He wanted to integrate these images with footage of Alexander seemingly addressing and manipulating the same faithful with mesmerizing oratory. It meant filming on a facsimile of the Nairobi stage against a "green screen," a special effect that allowed me to be instantly transferred from the cool of a LA studio to the heat and excitement of Africa.

My speech, penned by John Fasano, caught the precise flavor of Alexander's overweening megalomania, beginning in a wooing and cajoling mood, escalating into a furious diatribe underscored by thunder and flashlit by lightning, and finishing on a note of triumphant exaltation: "You cannot run from me — I am your light and salvation!" (Lightning fires from the sky. . .) "Yes, pray to your God. Pray to me!" (The enormous crowd falls in adulation at the stage. Satisfied, Stone smiles and looks up at his heavenly rival. . .) "Soon, soon all of your greatest creation will be mine. . . ."

It was enjoyable to flex Alexander's muscles once more and feel vocal cords again gearing up to grandiloquence. The scene safely captured, Larry rushed it off to Cannes where, it was hoped, a multitude of buyers and distributors would soon be kneeling at his feet to sample, as the accompanying PR material put it, a "wild, supernatural ride into the dark, nightmarish heart of the Great Tribulation and the end of the world as we know it."

Meanwhile I had some cajoling and orating of my own to accomplish. With the publication of the Shakespeare book, I embarked on a promotional tour that, if not quite as ambitious as Stone's global encirclings, seemed equally demanding and rewarding. Its scope had been further broadened as the start date of the movie had now been pushed back until late August 2000. There was no conflict with my other spiritual epic either, as this film had been postponed until next year.

My tour started in Hanover, the sylvan New Hampshire town where the book's publisher, Smith and Kraus, is based, as is Dartmouth College. Invited to speak there, I was also given the privilege of inspecting that other good book so crammed with history, poetry, and parable: Shakespeare's First Folio. Similar speaking and signing engagements followed in New York and Washington, including an enjoyable conference on "Shakespeare on Film" at the Newport Film Festival.

There, time slowed down to allow visits to the Breakers, Marble House, and other fabulous "cottages" that ennobled the shoreline. These palatial monuments to Mammon, built by a previous generation of global entrepreneurs to rival the great castles of Europe, had a panache and assurance that reflected Stone's own Hearst-like taste for domestic quarters.

After this enjoyable encounter with Robber Baron excess, I had an equally pleasurable brush with old Hollywood. As well as presenting an evening of "Music and Film" alongside Mickey Rooney, I found myself incarnating a dashing, inebriate Errol Flynn-type of movie star in *The Lot,* American Movie Classic's affectionate television valentine to the old studio system. It was also a homage to my own past, for I got to duel again and even to wear — in its third cinematic outing — my elegant camel-haired overcoat from *Murder on the Orient Express* that I had acquired after the wardrobe department of another film had fortuitously reunited us.

The *Megiddo* production office was to open on June 1st for the long and detailed preparation that such a complex film required. Our hopes were high: Its predecessor, according the *The Hollywood Reporter,* was the number four video in the nation. Finding a director was now a major consideration, and Matt and I discussed several options.

A friend suggested a director whom he respected both as a filmmaker and as a fencing partner. This was Brian Trenchard-Smith, an Anglo-Australian, who had once edited *Movie* magazine down under and had gone on to practice what he preached with a series of interesting and diverse films. "Proficient in foil, sabre and epee, he often gives fencing lessons on the set," his biography concluded. Although I had a sudden fantasy of any arguments about his direction being settled with a quick duel, he sounded ideal for the upcoming combat.

A demo reel of his work further impressed me, a reaction confirmed by viewing a pair of his recent films featuring two of my former co-stars — Ann-Margret and Jacqueline Bisset. As well as attractive work from the actors, Jackie's film *Britannic* had some powerful special effects achieved with economy and ingenuity — two factors essential for our modestly budgeted epic.

Brian turned out to share that quality of relaxed intelligence peculiar to other Aussie director friends, such as Bruce Beresford and Peter Weir. He was about my age, with sandy hair and eyes that wrinkled from amusement and living in the sun. He had laid-back, "no worries, mate" confidence as he outlined his concept of the film. Matt was won over, too, and with a blessing from Paul Crouch, Brian was engaged to lead us into battle.

He had insisted on several script revisions that were immediately implemented. The start of the film was now delayed until September, enabling me to accept other invitations for the summer that had been momentarily on hold. One was to the Galway Film Festival in Ireland, for the premier of *Borstal Boy,* a film based on Brendan Behan's autobiography that I had made the previous fall in Dublin. From there we went on to London and more book signings, including one in the sunshine by a silvery Thames, outside that restored monument to the greatness of man's creative genius, Shakespeare's Globe Theatre.

We also sat by a moonlit Thames on the terrace of the Houses of Parliament dining with new friends, John and

Norma Major. As Prime Minister, John was the authentic article, a born leader, but unlike Stone Alexander, he had based his authority on probity and legitimacy. He had fought in the Gulf War just as Alexander, who many equated with Saddam, would now fight his own Mid-Eastern war.

I had my own little brush with terrorism trying vainly to catch a train from a London station shut down by an IRA bomb — a real one, not a threat. Even tea at the Ritz, instead of being with my parents, was no compensation for the frustration — or the sickening speculation about what might have happened had this devilish slaughter of the innocents not been averted.

It was at this time that our key production members embarked on travels of their own. There was a "recce," or reconnaissance trip, for suitable locations, accommodations and local casting in Israel and Italy. From Rome, Brian sent me a postcard of a snow-covered Colosseum. "These conditions will probably not prevail during our forthcoming visit unless the real Antichrist shows up too," he noted, adding, "Movies and TV had not prepared me for the stunning beauty of the place wherever you look." There were also interviews in London to find my younger self, the adolescent Alexander.

Before Matt and Brian's departure, we all met up to discuss other cast choices. It has been said, with some justification, that correct casting does half of the director's job, and it is no accident that casting directors enjoy prominent screen credits. For the first time, Michael Biehn's name was mentioned for David, the brother. This was an interesting choice as, in a parallel and hugely successful role, Michael had stopped Arnold Schwarzenegger's *Terminator*, a creature as unconscionable as Alexander, from achieving his equally malign mission on earth.

The other key role was Stone's wife, now called Gabriella. I was reminded of her significance when attending a Hollywood function for President Clinton and the First Lady. Here was an Alexandrian scenario: The Leader of the World, charismatic, confident and admired, attended by his elegant, intelligent wife. Both nurtured their own agendas, but united in public to present a dazzling largesse. I made several useful mental notes.

It was now early August and I had some time on my hands before the start of filming in six weeks' time. After recording an audio book version of that other parable of goodness triumphing over evil, C.S. Lewis' *The Lion, The Witch and The Wardrobe,* I returned to my own current publication, the Shakespeare book. In a sort of basic training for the upcoming shoot, with its tiresome flights and anonymous hotels, I combined my book and my lecture tours and set off on the road again. I had specifically requested my lecture agency to include stops in Middle America, where support of *The Omega Code* had proved so crucial. "The fly-over people," as they are known on the snobbish coasts, provided a fascinating cross-section of this huge and diverse land.

Feeling as enthusiastic as Lucentio riding into Padua in my first film role, I trusted that what lay ahead would be neither a comedy of errors nor much ado about nothing, but all's well that ends well. Place names flashed by like minor characters out of Shakespeare: the French churchman, Notre Dame; the nobles, Boston and Rutland; the Roman, Chicago and the Greek, Minneapolis; and finally, that swarthy villain, Florida.

I had gone to Jacksonville both to sign books and to record a TV documentary, and here my wandering ways finally caught up with me. It had been the great summer of grounded and belated aircraft, and I had spent a good deal of it stuck in a succession of airport lounges wishing fervently that I had the ability to shape-shift like that effortless globe-trotter I was about to impersonate.

Now my exhaustion took a pathetic, even comic form. Wrapped only in a tiny towel, I was depositing my dinner tray outside yet another hotel room when, in a scene that would be dismissed as forced and improbable in a movie, the door sprang closed behind me, stranding me in the corridor. Pride is the one sin most unacceptable to Shakespeare and, swallowing mine, I was forced to take the long, crowded elevator ride down to an equally lively and curious lobby to gain help.

All this naked embarrassment had been caused by our film script! I had been couriered the latest rewrite, dated August 21st and now entitled simply *Megiddo*. Moved as much by curiosity as by conscientiousness, I had forsworn the post-shoot celebration at the bar and stayed in to give this latest version of the story my weary but unwavering attention. Once re-admitted to my room, I spent a good deal of that night making notes.

These were finished the next morning at the airport where, true to form, the plane returning me to LA had broken down after trying for an hour to take off. However, I was pleased to have this enforced interval free from phones and other intrusions, and even more delighted when the airline later sent me a check for $75 for my troubles.

"August 23rd, 2000. Notes made today on the trek westward," I wrote. "The structure of the film now seems to be in place." I particularly liked Brian's moving forward of Stone's meditation at Megiddo so that the sense of impending battle hangs like a black cloud over the entire movie. This transposition also paid tribute to Jean-Luc Godard's liberating observation that "A film should have a beginning, a middle and an end. But not necessarily in that order." "However character-wise," I continued, " some of the baby is in danger of being thrown away with the bathwater."

I was concerned that if he was the Antichrist, the young Stone should have an ageless omniscience and not be seen as an ordinary, vulnerable little boy. Also, the adolescent Stone was depicted as a violin virtuoso and I suggested this should be paid off in a later scene with the older Stone. It reminded me of a sequence cut from *The Omega Code* in which I had fiddled demonically on the Bracciano battlements. I asked Brian to review this outtake and see if it was usable here.

Above all, I wanted a stronger climactic scene between Alexander and Gabriella: "The scene at the moment is wet Kleenex whereas it should be striking sparks." I was also adamant that Stone's subsequent torture of Gabriella, when she eventually discovers the appalling truth about his identity, should not be physical, but mental — something much more cruel.

Although I admired the vigorous new dialogue, I sensed there was a constant danger of Stone ". . . morphing into a mobile mouthpiece for rhetoric. Unless he retains a measure of humanity he will be no threat, merely a demagogue. *Richard III* has been cited as a comparison — but what about Richard's ferocious delight in his own mischief-making? What about his sexy seduction of Lady Anne over the corpse of her husband?" Brian had envisioned a Shakespearean brio and panache in the rewrite, and I felt it was not there yet. Moreover, lurking at the back of my mind was John Wayne's cautionary advice to the actor: "Talk low, talk slow — and don't say too much."

Returning home, I found that Pat had interrupted work on an upcoming photographic exhibition in Hollywood to read the script. She had similar reservations: "I want the Devil to be, well, devilish — clever, amusing, and seductive," she explained. Over thirty years of marriage, I have learned to trust her insights, even if they are often delivered with all the disconcerting directness of an ex-New Yorker. I was pleased when Matt and Brian included her in the next script conference, along with Gary Bettman.

We met informally in the Spumante restaurant and, in the course of a delicious Italian meal — hopefully a foretaste of things to come — several interesting ideas developed. One was the concept of the young Stone meeting Raistlin, now called "The Guardian," in an initiation ceremony where the child breathes in the demonic forces that will, thereafter, energize his role. Diane Venora was mentioned as a possible Gabriella, which pleased me as I had recently admired her Gertrude in Michael Almereyda's Manhattan-based *Hamlet*. It felt good to be "in synch" as a team.

The next day I met with another key member of this team, the costume designer, Shawn Holly Cookson. As pretty as her name, she came armed with several racks full of clothes from which we selected the revised "look." Apparently the new design scheme was to depict Alexander's entire world in shades of red and green, while the "good guys" wore cooler blues and grays. This time blood was Stone's subliminal theme, and we chose shirts and ties in every variation of this hue. We also tried a new style of jacket, cut long like an elegant Edwardian banker's morning coat for, as Hamlet noted, "The Devil hath power to assume a pleasing shape."

I was now feeling fit for the fray and had this confirmed by the studio doctor who approved my medical insurance for the film. This was a routine checkup that I welcomed although, a confirmed homeopath and naturopath, I otherwise rarely patronize such orthodox practitioners. Ticking off so many "no's" on the long list of ailments was increasingly a pleasure.

CHAPTER THREE

Expeditionary Force

At the end of August, Pat and I left for Greece and a week of luxurious lotus-eating on a friend's yacht, sailing in the Ionian islands from Zakinthos to Corfu. We made a brief detour to Olympia where, modestly clad unlike the earlier naked competitors, I celebrated the integrity of my restored hip by running the length of the Olympic stadium. We sailed past a cape of this land of the gods where the world's fate had been decided in another climactic engagement. The ambitions of those other gods, Antony and Cleopatra, had been sunk at the battle of Actium, beneath the waves where we now cruised.

A fellow shipmate was Nicholas Gage, who had just published *Greek Fire,* a book about another great love affair that had ignited in this same crucible of history. It concerned a diva and an Alexander-like potentate — Maria Callas and Aristotle Onassis — whose liaison had also ended unhappily. I was reminded of a previous visit to Onassis' island base, Scorpios, and seeing his yacht *Christina,* their floating love-nest, abandoned at anchor like a mausoleum. "The gods are just, and of our pleasant vices / Make instruments to plague us," Shakespeare warns us. The word *hubris,* coined in these parts, came increasingly to mind as one pondered the fate of history's overreachers.

It was wonderful to enjoy this introspective calm and the boat's detached reality, though the modern world across the wine-dark sea encroached persistently through those infernal nuisances, cell phones, faxes, and e-mails. I learned that Michael Biehn was now set as David, and that Diane Venora was close to a commitment.

Even in these remote islands it was hard to escape the movies. Cephalonia was full of talk of the recent filming there of *Captain Corelli's Mandolin,* and I envied the film crew their paradisial location. I remembered, however, once filming a version of *Robinson Crusoe* for French television and, the envy of my friends, spending three months on various Caribbean islands. However, in perfect illustration of the maxim, "When the gods wish to punish us they answer prayers," Pat and I eventually longed for what had become a trial by pleasure to end.

It set me musing about the impact that films have on their hosts and I hoped that Bracciano, for example, would be better off for our renewed presence. This little town and its big neighbor Rome were now, I learned, to be our only foreign locations. Jerusalem and the real Megiddo site had been cancelled, mostly for budgetary reasons, though there was a growing concern caused by escalating Arab-Israeli hostility.

Hollywood even infiltrated the sun-washed sanctity of our yacht. At least three of us were reading *American Rhapsody* by Joe Eszterhas, the writer of that quintessential sex and violence film, *Showgirls.* With a gloss on recent presidential scandals and with a prurient rectitude, the book detailed his adventures in the film trade. Here, ironically amidst beaches full of unselfconciously topless bathers, it felt refreshing to be so far away from the kind of egocentric sleaziness that tarnished so much of our business. *Megiddo,* in contrast, seemed much less devilish — even pure and meaningful.

A slight but delicate air of scandal, however, lingered in Corfu where, at a party given by Jacob Rothschild, as the 1920s song went, I danced with the girl who danced with the Prince of Wales. Camilla Parker-Bowles, that Cleopatra of the Cotswolds, turned out to be, like Gabriella, an understated power behind the throne and was especially instrumental in getting us to Albania for the day. She was the houseguest of Lord Rothschild who was supervising an archeological dig in the ancient city of Butrint on the Albanian mainland across the strait. Like Megiddo, it had commanded this key strategic location since ancient times.

Camilla charmed the Corfu authorities into allowing us a brief, visa-less visit to the site — again the power of that inner circle of international authority on subtle display.

Butrint has a wonderfully preserved, acoustically impeccable, theater and I discussed arrangements to come back next summer — if plans for the opening *Megiddo* allowed — to perform there. Meanwhile, Albania remains the poorest country in Europe, a prime candidate for Chairman Alexander's politically motivated philanthropy.

On our long way home, the summer airline jinx struck again. Corfu was fogged in, stranding us with hundreds of anxious, overheated passengers in the tiny airport like extras in a disaster movie. There were no incoming flights to return us to Athens and on to the new world. Then, providentially, a little of that Camilla "celebrity" magic again worked its charm. I was recognized, and two seats on a packed German charter flight to Stuttgart were found for us. From there we hopped to Frankfurt and back into the arms of Lufthansa for its own Olympic marathon — a four-movie, forty-winks, and four-thousand-calorie flight to Los Angeles.

The next day, I was able to keep my scheduled appointment with Shawn for further costume fittings. The new Stygian colors looked impressive and the long-line jackets both flattering and interesting, especially when superbly cut in the latest Armani tuxedo. A conventional bow tie, though, seemed bourgeois and I suggested a flowing, Oscar Wilde-ish cravat for my first appearance in the film.

I wondered guiltily if my choice of clothes had been motivated subconsciously by their desirability as personal wardrobe after filming had finished, like my *Orient Express* overcoat. Stone's dove-gray suit from the first movie had already empowered several of my own speaking and social engagements, and his dazzling purple velvet jacket, if not exactly setting a new trend, had not gone unnoticed!

A monkish cowl, redolent with dark necromancy, to be worn by Stone in more meditative moments, was another costume suggestion. "And thus I clothe my naked villainy," Shakespeare's Richard III had similarly exulted, "and seem a saint when most I play the Devil."

Also, we agreed that I should wear a military uniform during the great Final Battle, and we improvised something there and then. An ensemble of a jacket festooned with gold-braided honors, jodhpurs, Sam Brown belt and beret was instantly effective and, not unsurprisingly, powerful — a hybrid of Goering and Mussolini. Boots completed the outfit, and I toyed with the idea of adding a baton or fly-whip, but I reluctantly dismissed these as excessive. We discussed including an overcoat — perhaps the fourth showing of my *Orient Express* apparel — as it could be chilly in October, but in the heat of an LA summer this was too exhausting to consider.

That evening I telephoned Brian with details of our sartorial innovations. His plan was also to endow the Beast with a demonic physiognomy based on my own features. I approved, believing strongly that, however terrifying, the character should retain some human traits, both vocal and physical. The film schedule, he now informed me, was a slimmed-down, muscular, power-packed ten weeks.

There was also an updated script awaiting me, and I was pleased that many suggestions had found their way into the new draft. The young Stone's meeting with the Guardian in a kind of Black Mass was especially effective.

I still had some reservations about Stone's return to Hell: The depiction of the netherworld seemed too literal, old-fashioned, and medieval. I felt that all our modern cinematic technology could create something never seen before and unprecedentedly terrifying. (My own favorite cinematic Hell was provided by the fiery furnaces of the Murano glassworks, roaring to Mozartian measures in Joseph Losey's enchanting film of *Don Giovanni*.) Nonetheless, I dashed off an enthusiastic fax to Brian: "I am sure that we will discover more exciting refinements as we progress within the arc you have fashioned. I look forward to getting down to work."

But first there was getting into shape by swimming or walking vigorously at least twice a day — I will do almost anything to avoid the sweaty confines of a gym, especially in LA, where people drive huge distances to walk on a treadmill or ride a stationary bike! However, in my early days as a raw recruit to his new National Theatre, my mentor and idol, Laurence Olivier, demonstrated by sheer physical example, often in the gym, the inextricable connection between performance and fitness.

There was just time, however, for one last long, indulgent soirée before succumbing to the impending ruthless regime of early rising and retiring. Placido Domingo, the new Artistic Director of the Los Angeles Opera, presented a gala performance of *Aida*. Afterward there was a glamourous *al fresco* dinner attended by all the black-tied movers and shakers of the city, a scene that would soon be duplicated in one of the castle rooms in Bracciano.

Placido himself is a role model of talent crossed with dedication, seeming to personify perpetual motion. Attending a previous performance of *Othello* in LA, we were puzzled to be asked to meet with him at the intermission rather than afterward. It turned out that, at the drop of the curtain, a helicopter was on the roof of the theater to whisk him to the airport and a waiting plane and on to Madrid where he resumed singing the next day!

I had recently been the Master of Ceremonies at a farewell concert for Peter Hemmings, the previous Opera Director, in which Placido and many of his stellar colleagues had performed. It had been astonishing, and somewhat moving, to witness the nervous tension still exhibited by some of the legendary performers. "Why do we do this?" and "There must be an easier way to earn a living!" were among the tortured moans to be heard before the curtain rose on yet another triumphant evening.

It reminded me that a certain high-strung tautness was an indispensable adjunct to any creative endeavor. I always welcome some nervousness before performing. The secret was to manipulate this pulse quickening to benefit, rather than compromise, the work. In a surge of empathy, my heart went out to the singers and musicians who had so dedicated their lives to embellishing those of their audience.

Nervous energy was certainly on furious display the next day when I returned to reality, revisiting Matt's office. His subterranean shelter was now transformed into a hotbed of almost radioactive intensity as the production geared up in earnest. Brian, however, seemed calm and rational under a constant barrage of questions. Asked about the *Omega Code* violin footage, he told me that he had reviewed it but would rather reshoot it as a linking sequence. He asked me to search the script for a suitable place.

I was introduced to Jerram Schwartz, Brian's First Assistant Director, who supervised his own hierarchy of assistants. His was one of the most important jobs on the set — setting a pace and concentration by cracking the whip so precisely that it energized rather than exhausted. The British, perhaps because of our long military history and culture of deference, are particularly adept at this, managing politeness without obsequiousness, and efficiency without effrontery.

Matt was his usual infectiously enthusiastic self, especially when describing his recent fortuitous discovery of the key Megiddo location — within commuting distance of where we now stood. He had hired a helicopter, he explained, for another film he was making, *Carmen the Champion.* Having some extra flight time in hand, he had used it to explore the hinterland of the city and in the middle of the Santa Clarita mountains north of LA, had discovered his own Promised Land, a facsimile of Israel's Jezreel Valley. The helicopter had swooped down to read the name of the property on a signpost: "Mystery Mesa."

I also met my "brother," Michael Biehn, for the first time. He had a coiled energy and dangerous intensity contrasted by kind eyes and a shy smile. We all made further suggestions about the script; in particular, I was anxious to finalize the big scene with Diane to be shot on the third day of filming. We then drove over to the venerable Park

Plaza Hotel where many of the interiors of *The Omega Code* were filmed and where this scene would also be staged — provisionally on the grand staircase.

The hotel ballroom, with its high beamed ceiling, was again serving as Alexander's office. Michael and I were rehearsing the scene we would first film when a phone call from Diane interrupted us. This was perhaps an appropriate foretaste of how Gabriella would come between the brothers in the film story, with catastrophic consequences. Diane sounded pleasant and committed, and we agreed to work together on "The Scene." Meanwhile, Michael and I, like wary boxers in an opening bout, continued to size up each other.

Later that evening Pat had an opening of another photographic exhibition, *What Piece of Work is Man?*, featuring her new and astonishing anatomization of cadavers, at a gallery in Hollywood. A thousand people attended; I was delighted to discover that among them was Brian's historian wife, Margaret, whose academic schedule would unfortunately prevent her from joining us in Italy for our own great historical re-enactment.

That weekend there was a rehearsal at Matt's house over-looking Universal Studios. Our young, aggressive David of an entertainer could thus size up his potential Goliath of a rival, especially from the house's "Omega Terrace," built on the success of that film. I finally met my new partner, Diane, and was impressed with her vivacious personality and understated elegance, so perfect for the "trophy wife," Gabriella Francini.

While Laurie plied us with refreshments, we gathered round her dining room table and spoke the words for the first time. Brian was infinitely courteous and patient with our demands, seeming very much in control of the material. We worked further on Gabriella's final scene with Stone, this time predicating it on the key word *love*, and also including reference to the dead and missing people who seemed to proliferate around him.

We also tried to make David's involvement more of a motivating factor, reinforcing the triangular nature of the relationship. Playing out an early manifestation of this, we all got down on the floor to enact the scene of Stone's murder of his father. It was a little too soon for such high-voltage emoting; I am certain that my own self-consciousness was shared by the others.

That evening Diane and I faxed each other versions of our ultimate scene, incorporating the original with discoveries from the rehearsal into a plausible sequence. I even managed to work in, "Oh, go to hell," a perhaps too obvious line, but one I needed to try out! We also fixed on a place for an embrace that would echo our characters' youthful passion. It would also symbolize a kiss of death, chilling and ambiguous, when Stone realizes that his wife, having eavesdropped on the previous scene with the world leaders, now knows too much.

It was at this time that I discovered an elegant leatherbound notebook that had been given to Pat and myself to record our Greek island cruise. "What I most regret in the particulars of my life," Jean-Jacques Rousseau once remarked, "is not having kept a journal of my travels." So, I decided to use this book to record another kind of voyage, the forthcoming cinematic odyssey through both familiar and unknown territory. Here hurricanes and fog would be as frequent as sunshine and balmy breezes, and any map of the journey would frequently be marked *terra incognita* as well as with that ominous and, in this case quite literal, warning, "Here be Dragons!"

CHAPTER FOUR

First Skirmishes

MONDAY, SEPTEMBER 11TH

The first day of filming. I'm not called to the set, so I spend the morning faxing more ideas back and forth with Diane to polish our scene, now convinced that it cannot be played as written. I'm mindful of an article in yesterday's Sunday paper about Helen Hunt, whose perfectionism is as notorious as her story-sense is acute. Apparently she will drive everyone crazy, beavering away at the script until it is in ideal shape. I determine, to some degree, to emulate this maddening but indispensable method. Besides, as a producer, even with a small *p,* I feel responsible for making my feelings known.

Working on the script prompts bizarre memories of filming in Canada in the late 1980s, a time when the local tax laws had transformed every other dentist and factotum into a film producer. An enthusiastic amateurism ruled over Montreal and Toronto, now metamorphosed into Hollywood North. In the spirit of the times, drugs were as easy to obtain there as morning coffee, but this was the least of our film's many problems. The script was unsatisfactory, and a new "writer" was engaged. However, when his improved version was finally delivered, all my dialogue had been left blank. When I remonstrated, I was informed, with the patience of someone talking to a child, that I was being paid enough money to supply my own words. At that point, all words failed me!

Now, in the swelteringly hot afternoon, I cross the hill to Beverly Hills, to the nearby Doheny Mansion that is serving as the grand Virginia home of Stone's father, Daniel Alexander. This splendid estate was built on the profits from the oil found locally in the late 1890s. There's now a financial gusher of another sort — filmmaking. I had worked here before when it stood in as the Seattle house of Joan Fontaine, my mother in a television film. My stepson, Rick, had studied here when it was the headquarters of the American Film Institute, and now its walls resound anew with the sounds of cinema.

Despite the lights it's cooler inside and, from the periphery, I watch a scene being filmed with Michael Biehn and David Hedison, our screen dad. All seems energetic and efficient. I marvel again at the size of this army of crew recruited to fight our war. Among them I recognize some *Omega* veterans and there are comradely reunions. I'm also introduced to new crew members, including Bert Dunk, the director of photography, who sports a rakish hat. During a break I show Brian the draft scene that, with the suggestion of another line, he approves. We're in business!

I'm never happy being redundant on a film set so, after watching a few more scenes, I leave. There is a whole second unit working independently in the garden, filming a shoot-out between the FBI and men loyal to President David Alexander who Stone has falsely discredited. All these blazing guns will probably guarantee us a PG rating — on the very first day, too! I just hope the weapons are not used in the advertising, an all too common Hollywood malpractice.

Living in a gun-toting society, after having been raised in a country that virtually bans them, is one of the few things that scares me about living in America. I find the humbug surrounding the plethora of school shootings, the earnest hand-wringing in full media spotlight, as nauseating as the violence itself. There's a huge national blind spot caused by a too-literal adherence to the word of the Constitution, even though one of its creators, James Madison, specifically warned that "In framing a system which we wish to last for ages, we should not lose sight of the changes which the ages will produce." I'm afraid that my old musketeer colleague, Charlton Heston, as President of the NRA, shares some of the blame for the legitimization and glamourization of so much contemporary violence. At least he should have the good grace to advocate muskets, not machine guns!

TUESDAY, SEPTEMBER 12TH

There are reports from the set about how good my child-hood self, played by young Gavin Fink, is turning out to be. Trying to incinerate his new baby brother, David, he's already setting a cracking pace in the satanic stakes. What luck! But now, can I ever live up to him? The thought makes me even more conscientious in learning my role for tomorrow.

Pat is now preparing for a major exhibition of her photographs in Ghent, Belgium, as part of the Flanders Film Festival. The house is knee-deep in them, but I am now quite used to clearing away graphic images of nudes and cadavers from the dining room table in order to eat. Selection is a tough job — how do you distill a lifetime of work into a few key, precious moments? It's like my being asked the impossible task of naming my favorite film. I wonder if Pat has a double standard, too. There's the work itself, and then the experience creating it when, sometimes, the latter can be more life-enhancing than the former.

WEDNESDAY, SEPTEMBER 13TH

My first day of filming. Hopefully, *this* one will be my favorite film. My end is my beginning: The first scene takes place on the same set in the Park Plaza Hotel where I finished the last scene of *The Omega Code*. A pleasing synchronicity. This time my office seems vaster and even more high-tech with a huge virtual reality screen dividing the room. Its display is blank, so in order to react to what will eventually be depicted there, Shakespeare's fundamental acting rule, "on your imaginary forces, work" is brought into immediate play.

The day is hotter, and the set is already an inferno — how appropriate for my character! I envy the crew their cool beachwear as I button up my wool suit for action. The scene with Michael goes well as my old alter ego, Stone Alexander, reports back for duty, cynical smile on lips and words honey-smooth. The only problem is that every other person seems to be called Michael, so a chorus of heads swivel in unison at the name.

By mid-morning, my brain seems to have separated from my skull in the suffocating air, and I think wistfully of cool Bracciano dungeons. A serpentine plastic pipe purports to pump cool air into the room, but like the castle heaters, its puny efforts have more a psychological than a realistic value.

Next, I work with the second unit. They ask me to deliver off-screen lines as if this is an imposition, but I insist it's indispensable — for both parties. It enables me to learn and color the lines and also, I hope, helps the performer on camera, more than when the script supervisor just speaks, rather than acts, the words. I try adding Chinese phrases to emphasize Stone's multilingual capabilities, but it sounds just like what it is — an add-on. I shall probably cut them when it's my turn to film the scene tomorrow.

The long, hot morning seems interminable, and I decline an invitation to postpone lunch and film an interview for the EPK (Electronic Press Kit). My guts are groaning for attention after their extra-early awakening and I head hungrily for the chow line. I'm high in the unlisted pecking order and so am allowed to jump the line — a desecration of democratic standards, but a practical one as I have to be back on camera in an hour's time in impeccable condition and without any postprandial slowing. It's too warm to eat outside in costume, so I retire to the whirling coolness of my trailer.

Dressing rooms and trailers are an indispensable part of any performance — they provide refuge not only for costume fittings and changes but also for essential contemplation and rehearsal. Recently they have become an amusing, and at times grotesque, reflection of "star" power — or rather, insecurity. I have marvelled at these bloated symbols of puissance — ballrooms on wheels, complete with kitchen and bathroom suites and sundry servants. I notice in film credits that some actors now have their "assistants." What on earth would I ask one to do? I have only recently allowed the alien presence of a cell phone to intrude into the studious calm of my modest, semidetached "double banger."

Lunchtime provides a free moment to check back in with the outside world. I call the production's travel coordinator to inform her of our plans for the upcoming trip to Italy. Pat intends to fly there via Brussels for her Ghent exhibition opening. I would like to stop over in England for the day for a brief reunion of my Oxford college's

Dramatic Society, and then join Pat, after which we would head down to Rome together. Is this being absurdly ambitious? Or is it just another healthy example of my cherished *carpe diem* philosophy, exemplified by an even longer-range plan to return from Italy via London, New York, and an upstate film festival? "I travel not to go anywhere," Robert Louis Stevenson encourages me, "but to go. I travel for travel's sake. The great affair is to move."

Such considerations are not quite as fanciful as they sound. Pat and I were once invited to a film premiere in prewar Beirut but declined, thinking that there would be ample opportunity to visit later. The city was then destroyed, and we never got to see it as the Paris of the Middle East. I resolved thereafter never to let such opportunities slip. At times, though, this can be daunting. Checking us in at the Los Angeles airport for a flight to a film festival in Bitola in the newly independent Balkan Republic of Macedonia, the agent refused to ticket our luggage, claiming that there was no such country!

In the afternoon I meet my shadow, Udo Kier, who is playing the Guardian. This is a natural addition to the spectral brotherhood of dark side roles, such as Dracula and Frankenstein, that already crowd his résumé. He has remarkable, piercing blue eyes and a ready wit. I like him immediately — especially when he confirms that unless the upcoming weeks of filming are going to be fun, then it's not worth the effort. He looks even more uncomfortable than I am in a thick black outfit that, thankfully, I rejected at the costume fitting. I leaven his distress by saying that he'll probably be grateful for it in the damp chills of Italy. Diane Venora's first scene is shot that afternoon. She looks just right in her costume and elegant chignon — vaguely foreign. I think she's going to be fun to work with too: I just wish we had more scenes together.

The heat intensifies inexorably and bottles of water are ferried in like a UN famine relief exercise. How prescient are Alexander's desalination plans for the world! I still cherish a plastic bottle marked "7th Stone Desalinated Drinking Water" from *The Omega Code*. Will it ever attain the value of Dorothy's red slippers from *The Wizard of Oz?* Meanwhile, I keep it alongside my souvenir "Y2K Emergency Storage Water." Emulating that old practice from the British Raj in India, however, I eschew all water on the set and drink one cup of boiling-hot tea after another.

Perhaps because of the heat, the shooting is taking longer than anticipated. Brian informs me that "The Scene" between Diane and myself will not be rushed but postponed until Italy when we can take advantage of the decor of the castle. Hooray! It also means more time to develop our relationship and to see what flows naturally from this. Diane is equally relieved.

Time presses and Udo and I are given the "bum's rush" — our last scene together is done in one hasty, schedule-saving shot. He's still working on a characterization, and I tell him that I hope we discover more in our relationship than is apparent on the page. Talking of which, there are some new revisions in which more of our suggestions have been incorporated. Good — the script is already taking on an organic life of its own. I return home exhausted, with an uncharacteristic headache.

THURSDAY, SEPTEMBER 14TH

The weather seems a trifle cooler although my headache still nags, making the ritual early-morning swim less enjoyable. It's odd having to come to a creative boil so early in the day; in the theater the reverse applies, with one's whole day being conditioned by the evening performance.

I meet up with Brian in my trailer to discuss the day's work — and to get to know each other better. I like his no-nonsense brand of direction, treating the actor as a colleague, not a pawn. His job can so easily cross the boundary from suggestion to coercion, and even further into forbidden sadistic realms. I reflect with distaste on the Brazilian director who filled his every shot with clouds of diffusing but choking smoke, and the games-playing Hollywood maestro who should have been wearing Alexander's dictator jodhpurs and jackboots. I envy Brian his shorts, which are now standard on the set, apart from us poor benighted, overdressed actors. My rayon shirt feels as if I'm wearing a plastic bag.

Udo and I film an extraordinary scene in which Alexander vomits a cloud of shape-shifting wasps that buzz his mischief worldwide. He and I agree that we have to "go for it."

There is no point in holding back and being decorous or self-conscious. This scene has to be horrifying! I appeal for inspiration to my inner child who, in this case, is like the fat boy in Dickens' *Pickwick Papers:* "I wants to make your flesh creep." We improvise a weird ceremony, culminating in a sort of satanic embrace where Udo breathes his malevolence into me — a flash forward from the scene where the Guardian initiates my younger self.

The wasps, incidentally, were originally scarabs, but Brian confesses that he changed them to something personally terrifying, having been stung by a wasp as a child. It's interesting how personal considerations influence things. Certainly insects are more familiar and comprehensible than more unimaginable mischief. Referring to the Holocaust, for example, the historian Raul Hilberg declared, "We can never get the full horror of such a subject if we strain to grasp it whole. The scale of a nightmare is often more accurately measured by its minutest detail." Perhaps even my concept of Hell is motivated by some childhood terror. I feel exhausted afterward from all the retching and vomiting, both on camera and off. Diane, however, has an even more complex task — how *do* you react when you discover that your husband is the Antichrist?

In contrast to all this extrovert behavior, I discuss with Udo the advantages of movie minimalism and mention the story of John Gielgud, filming *Chimes at Midnight* for Orson Welles. His role finished, he was about to leave for the airport when Welles requested him to pose for a few quick shots looking in various directions as if for a police "mug shot." In the completed film these neutral expressions, when cut together with a stronger image — like that of his dead son on the battlefield — are infinitely moving. The audience is left to interpolate an emotion.

I then reminisce about working with John Gielgud on the film of *Lost Horizon* when, swathed in furs and sweat, we trudged through the Burbank backlot Shangri-la during a similar scorching summer in a hail of plastic snow, valiantly pretending we were in the icy altitudes of the Himalayas. The film was generally dismissed by the critics, but it remains one of my favorites as it initiated a long friendship with a remarkable actor and most civilized man.

The temperature in the room is not diminishing despite

the addition of a more powerful air conditioner. How absurd that the Devil should confess that the heat is getting to him! We move on to the conference scene with the world leaders assembled in my office, in every variety of national dress. It brought to mind my own few meetings with global politicians — how humorless Mrs. Thatcher and Croatia's President Tudjman were, compared to the informal bonhomie of President Reagan and the formal niceness of Queen Elizabeth. Then, in every instance, it was the public face on display; this scene is about behind-the-mask *realpolitik,* the wheeling and dealing. Stone is a strategical optimist, like that other mesmerizing tyrant, Napoleon, who realized that "A leader is a dealer in hope."

I learn some phrases in Russian and Swahili to further spice up the international exchanges. I'm beginning to feel as grandly multilingual as that other world leader, the Emperor Charles V, who is reputed to have spoken Spanish to God, Italian to women, French to men, "and German to my horse." I feel for the small-part players who have no time to experiment their way into their roles, but who have to deliver on the spot. I try to treat them as colleagues. A certain discretion has to be exercised, though. I once smiled at a girl extra in a scene in Montreal, and she followed me all the way to LA to enquire if that smile portended more!

I suggest to Brian that I should notice Diane eavesdropping in the middle of the scene rather than at the end, so that there's an underlying and mounting tension. He agrees, and it works. I also use a huge amount of dialogue to get me from my desk down the length of the room to the door. Brian is appreciative and asks me to look out for other similar talk 'n' walk possibilities. I take this opportunity to compliment him on his comprehensive coverage of scenes — no doubt a by-product of his experience as an editor, knowing that, without this essential footage, lengthening or shortening a scene becomes impossible. We also resolve on a standard pronunciation of Megiddo, as "Megeedo" I trust this is not too Australian!

I'm not in the final scene and am glad to get out. Leaving the building, I notice our security guard being loudly harangued by a street person wearing a T-shirt marked "Jesus Loves." Tough love? And so, home; and like the great diarist Samuel Pepys, to bed.

Friday, September 15th

I'm not called and so can keep an appointment with Rex, my naturopathic physician. He confirms that I'm both dehydrated and mildly exhausted (after only two days!) and urges me to switch to drinks full of electrolytes.

What is worse, I wonder — filming in thermometer-busting heat or in a shivering excess of rain and cold. Certainly Britain can be infuriating for filmmakers, with the weather so capricious and unstable that it provides the main staple of conversation. Among my first films was Joseph Losey's *Accident,* made during the exceptionally sodden summer of 1966. One of its major scenes was a long languid Sunday party, much of it spent basking outside in summer "sunlight" provided by batteries of arc lamps — sometimes even at night when holes in the rain-soaked schedule *had* to be filled.

Heat can provide its own problems — and delightful remedies. Filming *The Island of Dr. Moreau* in the Caribbean in the mid-1970s, we arranged to start work in the cool of dawn, taking a long siesta and swim-filled break at midday when light was harsh and the sun as punishing as the cross-species torments inflicted on me by the good Dr. Burt Lancaster. Conversely the sword fights in Zeffirelli's *Romeo and Juliet* were done in conditions that Shakespeare perfectly described — "for now these hot days is the mad blood is stirring."

Later that morning I do some recording for the Oscar-winning documentarian Rick Trank, for his new film *In Search of Peace.* He startles me by announcing he's going to be married soon in the very ballroom where we have been filming, reminding me that it's not a hellhole but a most elegant, respectable venue!

SATURDAY, SEPTEMBER 16TH

Pat and I drive down to Temecula, a booming little town tucked in a mountain valley halfway between LA and San Diego where I'm to be given the Life Achievement Award of the Temecula Valley International Film Festival. It's another punishingly hot day — one of the most torrid that the region has experienced — and we stop in a refrigerated mall to cool off. A girl at the juice stand compliments me on *The Omega Code,* which I regard as a good omen.

We check into a hotel on a golf course that shimmers with heat. There's a surprise: Casper and Catherine have kindly consented to present the award. It's fun to see them again, looking even happier as Catherine confides that she is now pregnant. We reminisce happily about our *Omega* experiences over a promptly served dinner. Once, attending the Manila film festival in the Philippines, the banquet was so late in coming that, in a scene worthy of a horror movie, some ravenous guests fell upon and devoured the floral table decorations!

Improvising my speech, I pay tribute to the pioneering spirit of this enterprising town. It's hard to talk about a Life Achievement feeling that, rather than breasting the finishing tape, you are still very much in the race. Besides, as André Gide remarked, "Nothing is so silly as the expression of a man who is being complimented." I play on the word *life* and talk about the extraordinary quality of life that films have provided — the eye-opening travel, the chance to meet interesting people, and to see and interpret the world from a wider and more privileged perspective.

Our hotel room is charming, but it *is* another hotel room and it's too stifling to enjoy, so we drive home in the cool of the night bearing a handsome lucite trophy, some commemorative T-shirts, and several happy memories. I particularly relish the greeting sent by our son, Rick, from his own battlefront in Australia where he's producing the latest addition to the *Star Wars* saga.

Although not wishing to bite the hand that has so magnanimously fed me, I muse on the increasing proliferation of awards shows and their almost daily occurrence. Soon, it seems, everyone will be lauded for being a "Humanitarian," and there will be prizes just for the achievement of getting up in the morning.

SUNDAY, SEPTEMBER 17TH

Brian calls, croaking from a throat virus — occasioned, no doubt, by the feverish heat. Pat comes on line to preach her homeopathic gospel, but Brian is a confirmed antibioticist.

He compliments me on the work, which comforts me. Oh, how we actors like a little pat on the head — our achievement award for the day!

We discuss tomorrow's shoot. Apparently Udo won't be there for the scene in Africa because of a scheduling conflict; he'll be equally far afield filming something else in Vienna. Talk about shape-shifting! I reply that his absence won't matter as I have just announced to the World Union — in a prescient piece of improvisation — that I was making a *personal* world tour.

We review the dialogue exchanges in the very last battle sequences as they need to be finalized so that the cost of the computer generated "Beast" can be estimated. I agree to examine them anew and call Brian back. When I do so, he is in the middle of feeding his own little beast, a squirrel, and I'm delighted to learn that our director is sensible enough to take time out from the endless preparations and preoccupations.

Other possible changes are mentioned. I would like to see the Devil return to Hell in a much more defiant, Schwarzeneggerish, "I'll be back!" mode. I suspect, however, that this might sit uneasily with Paul Crouch, who would want none of these false heroics, and a more Biblically correct punishment. The commando raid at the end has been cut, Brian tells me, but I see this as positive. Now Stone and David can meet in a simpler, more personal *High Noon*-ish showdown. He also reports that Diane has been added to the Mexican village scene. A good idea: She deserves more to do.

I walk round the garden trying to learn my big speech for tomorrow, frightening the birds — and no doubt the squirrels — with my furious ranting. This evening I have been invited to present *Justine,* the film I made with my erstwhile Hollywood neighbor, George Cukor, at the Cinematheque. But I cancel: That was the past, I need to concentrate on the present. I pore over the map to find the best way to tomorrow's location in "Canyon Country." Join the movies and see the world!

CHAPTER FIVE

Into Battle

MONDAY, SEPTEMBER 18TH

Canyon Country turns out to be in the foothills of the high desert that rises northward toward Palmdale and the space shuttle's western home, Edwards Air Force Base. (One of the unexpected rewards of my job is that I once had the rare and thrilling good fortune to fly into orbit aboard the shuttle simulator while filming *Space* in Houston. The astronaut, Sally Ride, even gave me her vacuum-packed lunch, which remains treasured and uneaten.)

Our African and Mexican locations are together on a huge ranch reached along dusty roads to a base camp where the trailers have been circled like the wagons of yore. Remnants of the Old West are evident in words still current on film sets. Redolent of the crack of the whip and the jingle of harness, there's "teamster" for "driver." Wooden platforms are "apple boxes," conjuring up a vanished pastoral past of scented orchards, while "wranglers" handle performing beasts of the more conventional kind.

We are high up so it's relatively cool; but soon it's broiling in the breakfast line. Yesterday in Pasadena it reached a record 107°. It's so remote that cell phones malfunction, and there's only a Spanish-language station playing folk music on the radio — perfect for getting us in the mood for our south-of-the-border scene.

Diane is there looking Goya-esque in a new hairdo. She brings me some English tea, which instantly endears. We discuss her scene in the Mexican village. I'm concerned that her revamped character is in danger of becoming the reincarnation of Princess Di and Mother Theresa. The scene can't be too pious or preachy, I urge, or we won't cross over to that wider audience achieved in *The Omega Code*.

Seeing Pat's white straw Panama hat — a cousin of Bert

Dunk's signature one — which I have borrowed to keep the sun at bay, Shawn insists I make it part of my costume. The hat looks perfect with my long-jacketed suit in a vaguely tropical color.

Leaving the trailer at ten o'clock, I hit a wall of heat and force my way through it to the open-air stage. We are to refilm that "Africa" speech here on this other facsimile of the original Nairobi stage. As Brian and I work out the scene's physical parameters, it's like being fried alive. How could I possibly have felt so cold in Bracciano, or in Ireland last fall? Rehearsals are hastily completed and we start filming.

I feel quite mad and irrational. I welcome this as it can lead to an off-balance unpredictability that, with my character at least, is to be encouraged. At the back of my feverish mind echoes an astute observation made by Billy Wilder, with whom I had the good fortune to film *Fedora:* "An actor entering through the door, you've got nothing. But if he enters through the window, you've got a situation." So, even though it's providing precious shelter from the solar onslaught, I rip off my hat on the key word "chaos" and hurl it into the crowd. The extras, dressed like their Kenyan cousins, applaud spontaneously, which is always encouraging.

My vocal cords seem to dry up and I quaff copiously. Then, as Brian sets up a complex camera move where it sweeps through the crowd to finish on my outraged face, I suddenly become self-conscious and doubtful, suggesting that maybe a quieter, less scenery-chewing approach would be preferable. Brian, however, is adamant that my instinctive performance is correct. Besides, how can you address a crowd of a million people without heightened body language and high-pitched rhetoric? Thinking of Hitler at Nuremberg, I am reassured and continue my extrovert taunting of God. "*My* will be done!" I sneer.

A solicitous group of "no sweat" assistants are constantly at hand, proffering water, mopping makeup and changing damp clothing. It reminds me of filming *The Three Musketeers* in Madrid on a similar day, as hot as a Spanish Inquisition bonfire, and seeing the royal court ladies with heavy skirts rolled shamelessly to their thighs. It's now hotter than it was then and is supposed to stay this way all week. Perhaps God will not be mocked. But, thank God I learned the speech last night, before all my stressed synapses snapped shut. Now, at least, I know how Stone will react when he is cast back into Hell!

After lunch, Udo returns from Vienna bearing my favorite cake, an authentic Sacher torte so precious that it comes in its own wooden box. He shows me pictures of his weekend filming with Eddie Izzard, my favorite comedian. Udo is in amazing shape for such a swift round-trip. Michael Biehn also arrives and, in the welcome shade of some trees, we work out the action of our final confrontation for the special effects team so that, again, its cost can be estimated. Turning into a beast at this stage seems very remote and larky — like the first rehearsal of a play.

The final shot is the Mexican village — now with authentic tropical weather. The set is full of Hispanic extras who sit around chatting and enjoying themselves. Diane has literally let her hair down, but she still looks suitably noble ministering to a dying old lady. On the drive back, the canyons are beautiful in their twilit, Wagnerian other-worldliness. I'm so tired I keep losing my way and, on reaching home, fall instantly asleep as if drugged with some equally Wagnerian potion.

TUESDAY, SEPTEMBER 19TH

I'm not called today — which is just as well, as my sunburnt vocal cords are still in shock. Contacting friends at British Airways, I to try to free up my wait-listed seat to London. I also inform my college Dramatic Society that, even though it involves a swift commute from Heathrow to Oxford, I'm coming for the reunion.

WEDNESDAY, SEPTEMBER 20TH

Again, no filming for me, so I work on the new script that now sports multicolored page revisions. Past experience guarantees that, by the end of the shoot, it will be a veritable rainbow of paper. Pity the poor forest! But the new pages represent improvements. I'm relieved and optimistic that if we continue in this collaborative way, the script can only get better. I recall working on *Alfred the Great* with a distinguished actress who was so deeply disappointed with all her promised dialogue revisions that, in protest, she played her part as a mute!

The day is spent chained to my desk like Satan to the Fiery Lake, making more notes. Also, Shakespeare is scoured for suitable quotes, such as the one for Stone's eulogy to his father-in-law, General Francini, the head of the military academy: "Your honor calls you hence / And all the Gods go with you! / Upon your sword sit laurel victory."

Using appropriate lines from *Julius Caesar,* I also rework the speech to be delivered outside Rome's Colosseum and look for places where Gabriella can be integrated more into the action. I feel she could also stand up to Stone more, as she does in her teenage incarnation.

THURSDAY, SEPTEMBER 21ST

We're shooting tonight in the temple in Jerusalem — back at that Simi Valley Synagogue where my "coronation" scene in *The Omega Code* was filmed. By the time I arrive it's night and, even though I'm playing the Prince of Darkness, it feels too late for work. Handing over my notes, I'm pleased that they are welcomed. I also discuss further improvements with John Fasano. His young children are there too, and they present me with a "Three Musketeers" candy bar in return for signing their *Austin Powers* cards. It's so sweet to know that one has such youthful fans! Self-esteem is bolstered further when I'm told that the dailies look great. In fact, the lab reports that they are the best of their bunch.

We film the Black Mass where the adult Stone is introduced. Udo invents a Latin incantation, impressive until it is pointed out that he's intoning *pescadores* (fishermen) instead of *peccadores* (sins). We giggle like schoolboys in church, just as the audience at a performance of *A Midsummer Night's Dream* must have done when Shakespeare's immortal line "You spotted snake with double tongue" came out as "You potted snake with ham and tongue"! On the Shakespeare front, I try to emulate Henry V's exemplary behavior: "Nor doth he dedicate one jot of colour/ Unto the weary and all-watched night." However, I'm glad to eventually speed home in a fraction of the one-and-a-half hours it took me to crawl there in rush-hour traffic.

It's still a long enough drive, though, to review options and, by the time the car pulls into its garage, to have decided *not* to travel to Europe via London and Oxford. I realize that we will now be night-shooting until my departure and, if I feel so knackered after only one night's work, how will I fare after a whole week's worth? I resolve to emulate Pat and follow her directly to Brussels.

At home, I find her still high from the success of another gallery reception for her photographic exhibition. Another cinematic Stone — Oliver — was there and, admiring Pat's portrait of him, had apparently held his own lengthy reception under it. I'm so pleased for her — and proud.

FRIDAY, SEPTEMBER 22ND

Freak rain! It's all beginning to look like one of Alexander's curses on humanity. I'm T-I-R-E-D! Doing some filming for the Independent Film Channel, I just hope I don't look as haggard as I feel. We watch the Olympic games from Sydney. Now there's a show! Politics as athletics — a page from Stone's well-thumbed lexicon.

SATURDAY, SEPTEMBER 23RD

I start to learn Monday's scenes from a script constantly carried round with me. It's there when I'm shaving, and on my morning walk. I keep it in the car for rehearsal at stop lights (where I also write up this journal), and I am constantly astonished at the amount of useful time thereby accumulated. I'm immersed in the script when Brian calls, and I feel suitably virtuous. We discuss the rushes that he has just reviewed. Margaret, it seems, working at her computer, was uncharacteristically seduced into abandoning real history for make-believe to watch them too.

Brian tells me he's decided to stay in a motel near the location to save the more than two hours of commuting. I sympathize, although I rather enjoy the morning drive with the mind waking up and, when the biorhythms are in sync, flooding with fresh ideas. Even the return trip can be a necessary wind-down with the right traffic conditions and music on the radio. Also, I had seen enough alien hostelry during my Shakespeare summer. To echo Sir Andrew Aguecheek, "I had rather than forty pound I were at home."

Brian mentions the lens he plans to shoot with: one

used in wildlife filming that can keep both foreground and background in focus. Being focally in two places at the same time will, he assures me, help to sell the idea of Stone's omnipotence and omniscience.

Pat and I go to the Motion Picture Academy to see *Nurse Betty,* projected in ideal conditions and from a comfortable seat without the distractions of food and conversation. At first, I view it in terms of focus, lenses, and shots, but the film is so good that I'm soon seduced into forgetting all these extraneous issues and simply enjoy it.

MONDAY, SEPTEMBER 25TH

Off to the battle of Armageddon at last! First, there's a dawn dash along an arithmetic of freeways — the 101, to the 5, to the 14, and ever upward to Canyon Country. It's a terrain in transition, already being tamed into bourgeois respectability and infested with a raw rash of brand-new housing tracts. But there's still a residue of the Wild West in the bare, sculptured hills and limitless horizons. Eventually the road narrows to a trail and I arrive at our

Megiddo, the aptly named Mystery Mesa. The lofty view is extraordinary — it's exactly like looking across the Dead Sea to the mountains of Masada.

The mesa is five miles long and 1300 feet high. It used to be a wildlife refuge and, because of its remoteness, has never before been used for filming. There's a long, undulating, dust-plumed drive over its open, sun-burned surface to where the company is encamped, military-style, in camouflage tents. Tanks and guns are prominent, as are armies of extras already donning battle dress. "Once more unto the breach, dear friends!"

Since enlisting in the movies in the mid-1960s, I have done military service fighting an assortment of wars on behalf of various nations: from a fur-clad Viking chief to a leather-coated Nazi like Rommel, from a stiff-lipped pukkah British officer in the Raj to a Polish Jew in the Warsaw resistance. I've fought with sword and ray gun, underwater and in outer space, from zeppelins and from horseback, and I have maimed and killed more people than I care to remember. I've played as many goodies as baddies, but no one compares to the ultimate Baddie I now have on my hands!

In keeping with the ominous mood, a gritty wind is blowing — uncomfortable to work in but impressive on film. Clouds of dust added an impromptu and brilliant visual effect to my duels in the Zeffirelli *Romeo and Juliet* — they even brought in huge wind machines to duplicate it on calmer days. Now the gusts are particularly strong at the top of the hill where Stone's military headquarters — instantly dubbed "Stonehenge" — is located. There's even a throne from which he can survey and direct the battle.

It's a steep and difficult climb to the top and we are ferried back and forth from base camp. Brian has set up a scene where I arrive in Megiddo with a shepherd and a flock of sheep transiting the foreground, to give movement, as well as an authentic Middle Eastern touch. Bert, our cinematographer, has been here over the weekend to examine the play of light over the terrain in the course of the day. Conditions are now perfect.

Then it happens — a crane topples over on the narrow, precipitous track, almost severing a power cable. The driver is mercifully intact — more hurt pride than hurt limbs. Highlighting how dangerous location filming can be, especially on top of a remote hill, the incident holds us up. The heavy camera dolly, still in its truck, now has to be maneuvered out by a team of grips. We use this time for rehearsal — a windfall luxury! Brian confides that the film's already over budget and that some more days will be cut from the schedule. Another typical Billy Wilder remark comes to mind: "Nobody says — Boy, I must go and see that film. I hear it came in under budget!"

Black Monday continues its baleful sway after lunch. As I'm being driven back up the hill with Udo to play the scene I have been learning all weekend — Stone's meditation over Megiddo — we are handed a new version of the dialogue. I don't know whether to protest or even refuse, but I hold my peace because a hurried scan of the rewrite reveals that it might possibly be an improvement on the original. However, when filming, the undigested dialogue clogs and its rhythms are different, throwing me off balance. Udo is equally put out. There's awkwardness, too, with the military costume I donned hurriedly for the first time. The jodhpurs don't fit and the substitute trousers are inelegantly stuffed into the boots.

I drive home in a darkness as black as my mood. I don't feel I've done as well as I should with a key scene. Brian, however, has covered it well from many angles, so the miracle of editing might yet again be my savior.

TUESDAY, SEPTEMBER 26TH

It's still dark when I get up at 5:00 but my mood has lightened. Even at this hour the freeway exiting Canyon Country is jammed. What an irony — all these people who escaped the gridlock of LA are now enmeshed in their own local equivalent. There is a magnificent sunrise over the mesa reminding me of all those other location dawns — in India, Australia, Brazil, Israel, and, particularly, in North Africa. Pat and I once spent the night with Juliet Greco in a Moroccan fort deep in the Sahara and were awakened by the soldiers to witness a spectacle unparalleled in its awesome beauty: The crystalline night sky stained shades of burnished red and orange. I can understand why the desert has such a strong religious significance.

Filming gets off to a cracking, disciplined start. Michael

Biehn and I trim down our final confrontation scene in order to make up for yesterday's lost time. There are still opportunities to chat, though, and I learn more about him. He tells me about his family — he has sons too. Also, he has never been to Italy, and I envy him the first impressions his impending trip is bound to make.

I have brought an umbrella with me, and don't care how improbable or foolish I look striding around with it like a camp version of *Il Duce*. It's hot and there's no shade! Lunch is literally hours away and we stave off the pangs with frequent visits to the craft service table. When I started out, this was modestly furnished with doughnuts and sticky buns, with a few nuts and carrot sticks for the health conscious. It has now bloated into a permanent feast, including cappuccino and hors d'oeuvres.

Lunchtime finally arrives and there's a mad descent to the "roach coach." But this fleeting hour is also essential for office work. Fortunately I'm thwarted, as the broiling heat in the car has immobilized my cell phone. I'm even more grateful for my peaceful, cool retreat.

After lunch, Udo and I are not filming and so work on

an upcoming, rather straightforward scene where we video-conference with the Israeli Prime Minister. Trying to pump some energy and interest into it, I donate Udo some of my lines and play the scene furiously while he remains icy calm. Udo and I are the same age and reminisce nostalgically about London and its swinging sixties' film scene. He has retained that era's irreverent sense of fun along with some of the patois. "Working!" he will invariably respond with a curious blend of guilt and indignation whenever his name is called. We present our final, fully rehearsed version to Brian who approves it, and it's the last sequence we film.

Arriving home in a near-catatonic state, I find that Pat has brought a friend back from viewing her exhibition. I go through the motions of making polite conversation, but I'm not that good an actor and am sent off to bath and bed.

WEDNESDAY, SEPTEMBER 27TH

The morning is free until 11:00 as we are filming half-day and half-night, which is far preferable to the stress of working all night. I spend most of it making travel plans — for a book signing in Brussels and that film festival in upstate New York. I'm also secretary for an absent Pat — and am very efficient; all her telephone messages are lined up as neatly as Stones's battalions on the hall table when I leave.

A thick, cool, marine mist still shrouds the sun, but it clears as soon as I arrive on location. But the light is now different — more diffuse. How lucky that we filmed our wide, panoramic shots when it was perfect, making the distant mountains look like the richly hued background of an old master painting. I feel unaccountably gung ho — which is good for the scene where I preen, taunt, and crow over the captured Michael Biehn in his prison pit.

The sun is soon doing its own malicious taunting. Brian wears a large coolie hat with his nose whitened like a surfer's making him look almost as ridiculous as I do with my parasol — especially today, a major macho, testosterone field day. There are battlefield detonations orchestrated by Paul Lombardi, one of the best special effects technicians in his explosive business. Not going to Israel has enabled us to avail ourselves of Hollywood's finest.

Paul, surrounded by the bizarre pyrotechnical tools of

his trade, cautions that the wind might be a problem — it could suck the exploding mixture of propane gas and titanium into the set. Now *that* would be an extra special effect! The fireworks prove spectacular; smoke hangs over the battlefield as it did over LA during the infamous Rodney King riots when one of my more apocalyptically minded neighbors invited me to "bring my guns" and join in a communal barricade of our street.

The focus puller tells me that his father worked on the special effects for *Logan's Run* and was burned for real in the carousel sequence. After sympathizing and sending good wishes, I tell him how glad I was that the effects didn't overwhelm that film so that emphasis remained on the story. *Logan's Run,* coincidentally, was on television last night and several of the crew amaze me by telling me that they watched it. Where on earth do they get the energy? But at least they are young — unlike Logan and his fellow runners, their palm lights are not blinking "Last Day." They assure me that the film holds up well — and didn't put them to sleep.

Rob Bredow, our youthful visual effects wizard, is so

fresh-faced and polite it seems he couldn't hurt a fly, let alone manufacture monstrous man-eating insects. He shows me some sketches of how they plan to turn me into the Beast — it all looks very ambitious, scary, and exciting. There is a call from Pat who is finalizing the Byzantine negotiations of my contract. I am happy to let her do this as she has a talent for it, with an instinctive knack for reading — and understanding — even the smallest print and asking the obscurest questions. Over the years she has saved us a small fortune. My lawyer was so impressed that he once asked her to join his firm!

The afternoon filming is a race against the dying golden light, and the work is fast and productive. At one point an enormous explosion detonates just as Udo is about to speak — it's the closest illustration I have seen of someone "jumping out of their skin." Despite the pressure — or perhaps because of it — I'm ashamed to say I laugh uncontrollably.

Learning to suppress laughter during a performance is one of the essential tasks an actor has to accomplish. At the National Theatre in London, I've seen the noblest knights and dames of my trade be paralyzed by some stupid incident and have to turn upstage to mask their hilarity. In England it's called "corpsing," presumably after all the corpses left lying around for too long in Act 5 that invariably find something amusing that sets them shaking uncontrollably. It's a highly infectious disease and can incapacitate an entire company as surely as if laughing gas had been pumped in from the wings.

It's not new, either. There's a charming story told about the great eighteenth-century actor, David Garrick who, during a performance in London one very hot evening, had to halt in mid-scene and rush off stage. A fat, over-heated gentleman in the front row had apparently removed his large wig and put it on his mastiff seated beside him, and the sight of the bewigged dog staring earnestly at Garrick had proved insuperable!

At the meal-break I encounter John Fasano and we discuss the film's ending that will be shot tonight. Concerned that the Beast should retain a measure of "humanity," I even suggest he should morph back into human shape for the last desperate supplication to his heavenly rival. Realistically, though, this is too expensive an indulgence.

We chat about a new film in which my old *Austin Powers* co-star, Elizabeth Hurley, has graduated — or been relegated — to playing the Devil. A hugely expensive giant puppet of her, like the rejected idea for Stone's cloned Golem figure, was apparently scrapped, presumably for the same reason that Satan is more seductive in human shape — and certainly in Elizabeth's. I determine to bear all this in mind during our next crucial bit of filming, even though now it's only my voice that will be performing.

The night shooting begins; we're in for a long and tedious time as the special effects require patience and precision. The team who are about to turn me into a monster are as assured as they are young. They are masters of the new digital moviemaking — exemplified by Ridley Scott's *Gladiator.* In that film ancient Rome was created with clicks on a keyboard, and my dear comrade-in-arms, Oliver Reed, who joined his own Creator for a drink and an arm wrestle before his role was finished, was able to complete it thanks to many of the techniques that we are using tonight.

The modus operandi is to first film a "plate" shot of the scene minus actors, and then one of myself performing an approximation of the lines, so that my facial expressions can be duplicated in the animation. Michael Biehn, meanwhile, has to react as if menaced by the Beast. At one point, a huge prop devil's claw grabs him by the throat, hurling him to the ground in a backward fall that is doubled by a trampoline-launched stuntman. Then the scene is filmed again, this time with my role being taken by a man in a bright green body suit wearing a cap with a large protrusion approximating the nine-foot height and wingspan of the Beast. "The Jolly Green Giant," as this individual is inevitably called, becomes the butt of endless jokes, which he takes with a forbearance worthy of his stature. It's all very surreal and time-consuming, yet very necessary.

Udo keeps consulting his watch like an anxious producer, as he has to be finished off tonight so that he can fly back tomorrow to Vienna and the Eddie Izzard film and, no doubt, more Sacher torte. I wonder when I'll find time to pack; Udo and I discuss the tempting logistics of travelling to Rome with no luggage at all and buying an entirely new designer wardrobe there. I tell him to look out for Pat who's on his same Lufthansa flight, en route to Brussels and Ghent.

My own immediate travel plans are reduced to a hobble when, at one point in the night on Bald Mountain, I slip on the gravel slope and come crashing down. Protecting my hip, I fall heavily on my arm. I feel shaken but otherwise all right, and telephone Pat who sets about arranging a chiropractic treatment tomorrow. At the wrap, I speed home on totally deserted streets in a heart-stopping, illegal forty minutes.

THURSDAY, SEPTEMBER 28TH

I rise at 7:00 to find I can't raise my arm without pain. Fortunately, Pat has arranged a session with Dr. Marc Pick, my chiropractor and her partner in all her extraordinary photographic anatomization of body parts. A magical hour of manipulation ensues, and I feel grateful for the gentle unkinking. Marc tells me how lucky I am: Only muscle is damaged and a vertebra misplaced. I pick up a message in the car to say that the call has been postponed until 1:00 PM. Hooray!

Once home, Pat and I race around each other in a double whirlwind of activity. I manage to rebook myself on a later flight so I won't have to leave for the airport at 1:00 PM tomorrow, only a few hours after filming all night. I bid farewell to my wife to the sound of a continuously ringing phone, collecting the messages to return them on the long drive to work — thankful that this distracting practice is still not illegal.

Back at base I discuss the upcoming scene with Brian by two-way radio; he's already up on Stonehenge preparing to blow it to pieces in the Final Battle. The script has Stone emerging from this firestorm with his uniform shredded and smoking, but otherwise physically intact. I opine that this might be misinterpreted as a makeup mistake or, worse still, that I'm too much of a prima donna to get messed up.

I suggest that Stone emerge from the conflagration totally untouched, with a line to David, "Now you know who I am." Brian buys it and, while getting dressed, I think of prefacing this with "Surprise!," in sardonic echo of David's same greeting when we first meet at Stonehenge. This is the way we film it. Later I consider following up on my earlier note about reworking my final dialogue when overwhelmed by the Deity's white light, so that it's more a devious challenge and less an abject plea. But no doubt this would infringe on strict scriptural directives.

Pat calls from the airport to say a final good-bye. Standing on this windswept plain, I can't believe I'll be on the same flight in twenty-four hours' time. At 2:00 PM there's another meal and I fuel up on two helpings of hot peach cobbler. We resume filming and the remote technicrane camera — indispensable in this rough terrain — jams.

Again, this technical hitch turns out to be fortuitous as the enforced idlement gives me the chance to speak to Rob, the visual effects guru, about the upcoming dialogue for Stone's beastly transformation. He suggests bringing certain lines forward, such as the litany of satanic names, to be intoned as Stone's body bursts open to reveal his true identity. We agree, and that is also exactly how we film it when the camera deigns to co-operate some time later — accidentally, or on purpose? Around 4:00 AM I'm finally sent to Hell — and on to home.

I "sleep" until 9:00 and go instantly into manic overdrive. There are so many things to do: packing seems the least of them. Pat, in her endless quest for optimum natural health, has left me a newly purchased solar watch that has been treated to ground and balance the body, using a gravitational technology spelled out in several pages of accompanying literature. It works — I feel enormously energetic and concentrated. (Even if it's only the placebo effect, I'm impressed!)

Going about the ritual business of shutting down the house for a month, I stop the newspapers, top up the pool and enjoy a last swim. Instructions in approximate Spanish are left with Elisa, our indefatigable housekeeper, whose only complaint is that we leave her too frequently. It's the first day I haven't really thought about the film — but I'm sure it's still roiling away in the subconscious.

Pat calls from Ghent. She missed her connection to Brussels by three minutes. But she's slept for eight hours: Those reclining seats — costly enough to banish all thought of slumber — are well worth their expense. She asks me to bring her raincoat as it's pouring there. My Shakespeare book co-author, Adrian Brine, sends a fax finalizing a restaurant for our rendezvous in Brussels with a local journalist, and requesting my Italian itinerary. Another fax follows my response, commenting that Bracciano sounds like a character in a Webster play! Adrian concludes with an appropriate Shakespearean flourish: "Flights of aircraft sing thee to thy rest."

CHAPTER SIX

Invasions

FRIDAY, SEPTEMBER 29TH

Off to the airport at 7:30 PM; it's pleasant to be chauffeur-driven after so much solo commuting. A residue of that old childish excitement about flying remains. I always get a window seat and never cease to experience some thrill at being airborne. A psychic once told me that, in a past life, I assisted Leonardo Da Vinci with his glider experiments, so perhaps that explains it!

SATURDAY, SEPTEMBER 30TH

I snooze my way to Frankfurt and feel *wunderbar* — and even better after a shower and shave. I recall a less cosy arrival here on a Pan Am flight from India in the mid-1970s, a time when airline hijackings were almost daily in the news. I had been invited to experience the landing from the cockpit. At the time, my hair and beard were long for playing John the Baptist. Spotting my hirsute figure hunched behind the pilot and, assuming I was yet another hijacker, the control tower alerted the police, who surrounded the plane with guns drawn and pointing at me.

All there is to kill now is time, and I squander it on the newspapers. One headline reads, "Second Day of Violence at Jerusalem Site," making me thankful for the prescient decision not to film there. I also telephone my Oxford college where the University Players reunion is just concluding with tea in the Master's lodge.

I speak warmly to my old tutor, Peter Bayley, who was once inveigled into playing a moving Cardinal Wolsey in our student production of *A Man for All Seasons*. I say how much I regret missing the college's 750th anniversary celebrations, and how I had once discussed coming to the big party with another former college undergraduate, Bill Clinton. For a fleeting time, I entertained fantasies of us both flying in on Air Force One, the same plane whose facsimile we have already used as a set for our President David Alexander in *Megiddo*.

It's night by the time I arrive in Brussels. The airport looks worn and shabby — hardly a fitting first impression for the nerve center of the new Europe. There's also a distinctly continental *pissoir* smell in the loo, one I recall from childhood, along with memories of sugared crepes and incomparable *frites* and epic crossings on the storm-bucking, vomit-sprayed Channel ferry to Ostende in days when flying was for the few.

A film festival driver awaits me. His car is modest compared to the dazzling white stretch limo that once picked up Pat and myself at a deserted Zagreb airport, in the middle of the Balkan war, when filming *Gospa* with Martin Sheen. Remonstrating as to its suitability — especially as a bomb target — we were told that the film's producers wanted us to feel at home and to ride in our accustomed

Hollywood style. It felt too churlish and ungracious to point out that we *never* used such pompous means of transportation!

Pat is there in the Sofitel, a modern hotel in the core of an older building opposite the Town Hall with its Gothic facade spread out like a fantastic stone tapestry. She insists I bathe while still wearing the new solar watch, claiming that it energizes the water, repairs DNA, and banishes jet lag. And I believe her! I've certainly never had as much energy since first putting it on yesterday.

SUNDAY, OCTOBER 1ST

We head to Pat's exhibition at St. Peter's Abbey — a wonderful space with a high vaulted roof, huge windows, and her photographs arranged around its walls like so many altarpieces. Her work comprises the usual triptych of celebrities, nude studies of people at work, and cadavers. I revisit my movie past — there are portraits of former colleagues including Sean Connery, Peter Ustinov, Liza Minnelli, Liv Ullmann, and Bob Fosse.

Pat told me that Fosse was the most concentrated person

she had ever captured on film; you can see his eyes behind the constant wreath of smoke glittering with almost manic intensity. I recall my first meeting with him in London at an audition for *Cabaret*. Again, I had just flown in overnight, this time from Puerto Rico. It was the beginning of an incomparable working experience. Bob was not without his "devilish" qualities, usually goading himself mercilessly to even greater artistic achievement.

Michel Piccoli and I are depicted romping around Morocco in a Philippe de Broca comedy. We all became firm friends; at one point Michel and I even put local kohl on our eyes to out-sparkle our leading lady, who was proving to be, as the French might say, a *douleur* in the *derrière*. There's also an image of another friend and traveller, Tennessee Williams, sitting on his suitcase at the New Haven station during our tryout for his play, *Outcry*, his trusty typewriter beside him. "Make voyages — attempt them," Tennessee had encouraged, "there's nothing else!"

There are formal speeches to the assembly of dignitaries including an elegant one from my wife, who I'm sure was even then entertaining the possibility of photographing the

Mayor stark naked at the microphone. At lunch we discuss the peculiarities of the Flemish language, which, apparently, is spoken with the same huge differences of accent within short distances as happens in England. "Flemish is less a language, more a throat disease," one of our hosts volunteers.

We visit the Modern Art Museum where there's a one-second film by Marcel Broodthaers — the shortest on record, with barely time for this great surrealist to sign his initials. I love this fantasy in the Belgian character, so different from their sensible cousins, the Dutch. Perhaps it's due to the Catholic heritage here, as opposed to the stricter Calvinism of their northern neighbors.

It has been a day of being "on" and, despite our watches, jet lag exerts its own surreal mind-game. We decide to stay in and enjoy one of the real pleasures of hotel living — room service replete with the great national dish, *waterzooi,* a sort of watery chicken stew. There's no escape — *Alfred the Great* is playing on the television and, with some amusement, we watch my younger self, raping and pillaging as the Viking King, Guthrum.

Despite its title, it's not the greatest film — but it did once save our lives when we were mugged in Rio de Janeiro. Surrounded by six knife-wielding thugs, I thundered at the top of my voice the Danish battle cry, only to see our assailants retreat into the night like so many scared Saxons!

Pat and I shamelessly pillage the large box of chocolates that has been left in the room.

MONDAY, OCTOBER 2ND

Pat gives a television interview in the empty abbey. Sun pours in, projecting windows of light on the floor, and I enjoy the calm and beauty. There's a chance now to look at the exhibition in detail, something impossible at crowded openings. Pat's juxtaposition of images — eyes both lively and lifeless; bodies, glamorous as well as inanimate — makes for poignant viewing. One's aware of the Websterian "skull beneath the skin." By coincidence, workmen digging in the cloister outside unearth a thirteenth century skeleton — it would look quite at home here!

TUESDAY, OCTOBER 3RD

Back to Brussels and a reunion with Adrian at lunch with Philip Thirard, a Belgian arts journalist who has asked to translate our Shakespeare book into French. Afterwards, there's a book signing at Waterstone's store in the city center. It's like an informal party; many friends show up, and because Adrian is a hugely popular and influential director in Belgium, many other actors and directors. Like this one, my visits to Brussels have been usually fleeting and infrequent, although I was here in the early 90s filming *Eline Vere,* based on the great Dutch novel, and enjoyed the city as a film set.

On the flight down to Rome the caterers are on strike, so there's no food; this is just as well, considering all our recent chocolate chomping. Another strike during an intermission at Rome's Teatro Sistina in the early 1960s, when I was touring with Britain's newly formed National Youth Theatre in *Julius Caesar,* comes to mind. It lasted so long that the real enraged Roman mob made our staged one seem puny indeed.

We are back in the Grand Hotel Plaza in an imposing suite that could have been the set of some Visconti epic and seems entirely in Stone Alexander's grandiose taste. Nothing has changed. The big bronze key that admits us is still on its unloseable rod, the size of a field marshal's baton. There's the same spacious terrace overlooking the Via del Corso and an incomparable panorama of roofs and monuments. Within, there's a huge marble mausoleum of a bath with antique accoutrements.

What's new is a script, just arrived from my agent. An unread screenplay is always a tantalizing object. It could be the one that sets the pulse racing or the spirits drooping, its destination either the desk or the wastepaper basket. It could be the project that sends one to some unknown, exotic part of the world — or even changes one's life. My fingers toy tantalizingly over the sealed envelope, but I decide to do the right thing and give my undivided attention to our present script. Lines are dutifully learned before lights out at 1:00 AM.

WEDNESDAY, OCTOBER 4TH

The dapper hotel manager greets us and welcomes us back for breakfast in the gilded, mirrored, and velvet-swagged ballroom. It was decorated by Renzo Mongiardino, who designed the equally sumptuous sets of *Shrew* and *Romeo and Juliet.* I keep expecting to see Claudia Cardinale encircled in a crinoline and the arms of Burt Lancaster, come waltzing by the buffet table that groans with everything from cheese to chocolate cake. The newspapers report the worsening situation in Israel and Pat remarks to Larry Mortoff how fortunate it is that we are not filming there. "But think of all that free production value, all those tanks and guns!" he replies. Producers!

Matt tells me that his boys are being tutored on the Internet, in addition to the incredible liberal arts education they are absorbing just by being here in Italy. I first came here as a similar young schoolboy, staying in *pensiones* and crossing the country by coach. The exposure to so much art, both in the street and in the museum, made an unforgettable impression. I also remember the thrill of riding the clanking trams that had by then disappeared from London.

Decades later they are still in Rome, but now gliding by, transformed into shiny, high-tech conveyances like those tube cars in *Logan's Run.*

The morning is well spent on demagoguery — I on the terrace, working on Alexander's Colosseum speech, and Pat inside watching a replay of last night's first presidential debate on CNN. I'm glad to learn that Gore has some of Alexander's telegenic brilliance — but does he also have his killer instinct?

We walk across Rome to Trastevere, for lunch at Sabatini's. The scaffolding is now gone and the city looks magnificent after its millennial cleanup. Sadly, there's still graffiti everywhere, as in pre-Giuliani New York. If I were Alexander, or even the American president, I would cut off offenders' hands! We dine in the Piazza Santa Maria, opposite the church with its twelfth-century frescos, while musicians serenade us sentimentally as if we're tourists. This is show business too, I realize, but I'm grateful when they are shooed away, restoring the square to its ancient serenity.

Back in the land of the lira, the brain-challenging business of reckoning every purchase in thousands, even millions, is renewed. It's enjoyable, however, to speak Italian again, a skill acquired on my first film here, and improved on every subsequent encounter. Even the food sounds better in its native tongue. It's certainly delicious here, making us happy to sign the guest book and pose for photos with the waiters before strolling back in the sunshine to the hotel.

There I finally pry open the new screenplay to reveal my fate. You can usually tell the quality of a script by its first few pages, and this one has me turning them, like Stephan's *Megiddo* outline, with mounting enthusiasm. It will film in England — certainly no hardship — and I call my agent with a positive response.

The luncheon pasta is still weighing heavy, so we take a light supper of fruit while perusing the information sheet that the Italian co-producers have prepared. It's full of charming cross-cultural gems, including a description of the Via Giulia as "the reinnassimental street of the city, full of foreshortenings and images surely among the most pregnant of Rome."

The flowers in the dusky room exude a sensual, southern perfume as we are serenaded again, this time by swallows animating the orange evening sky.

THURSDAY, OCTOBER 5TH

Up at 6:00. The ballroom is in the process of being transformed into a Scientology convention center; various devotees of this faith join us in the breakfast congregation. Afterwards, Michael Biehn and I drive up Monte Mario in the pearly morning light to the Villa Miami — the new set for Alexander's Roman HQ.

It's an improvement on its predecessor, with stunning panoramic views over the still-awakening city. I think of the statue of Christ being helicoptered over Rome in Fellini's *8½* and wish we could duplicate that stunning symbol with one of Alexander, similarly transported. Many of the crew from previous movies are present. There's Stephano, the makeup artist who transformed me for *Jesus of Nazareth,* who confides that the film was an equally powerful experience in his life, too.

We film the fatal handshake whereby Stone kills the US President, played by Lee Ermey, the quintessence of crewcut, good ol' boy patriotism. I'm the quintessence of vanity as I've asked Rena, the makeup girl, to give my hand a manicure for its big close-up. Also on camera is Larry

Mortoff who, with his FBI earpiece, looks startlingly authentic as a security agent. Lee, unforgettable as the gunnery sergeant in Stanley Kubrik's *Full Metal Jacket,* is as friendly as he is imposing, though I keep expecting him to tell me to drop and give him fifty.

Filming goes well. We're rewarded with *cestini,* box lunches that bulge with gastronomic goodies, recalling cine cuisine elsewhere. There were the meager soups served in Communist countries, and the exquisite lacquer boxes in Japan, where our bolshy British grips rebelled at being given rice not doused in sugar and custard! I also remember the folly of a producer friend of mine who, wanting to reward his hardworking crew, served them haute cuisine when all they wanted was basic grub.

Udo arrives back from Vienna with further reports of his Eddie Izzard film in which he plays a Nazi. I wonder what it must feel like for him, a German, to continually play such parts — it's like us Brits being portrayed in America as ascot-wearing toffs. Udo confesses that he had given the Nazi salute, but all photos of it were *verboten.* I meet Noah Huntley, my adolescent incarnation, who has just arrived from London. We have a certain physical similarity, apart from his lack of a broken nose, but I wonder if Noah shares the same excitement I felt at being in his place thirty-five years ago, filming in Rome for the first time.

Pat arrives and within moments I know everything that's going on behind the scenes. She has the gift of empathy and people unburden to her instantly and liberally. She would make the perfect talk-show host — or international spy. Pat is, in fact, doing some spying of her own. She has been asked to direct a movie of a script she wrote and has been assiduously studying cinema both in class and on the set. Pat now learns that our present film schedule has again been revised, making our intended return to Ghent for the film festival and further publicity for her show problematic — at least for me. "A wise traveller has no fixed plans," Lao Tzu sagely consoles, "and is not intent upon arriving."

In the afternoon we move to our adjoining set, the Café Zodiaco overlooking the city and a big bend in the Tiber. The restaurant has been bought out by the production for the filming, but patrons still come — and are served. We all watch Noah romance young Gabriella, in the beautiful shape of Elisa Scialpi, sweeping her off on a Vespa. I tell Udo I have a premonition that, as our "bowl of wrath" scene is a dusk shot, there will be no time to rehearse. As before, we swap and re-jig lines, working up a routine with wine glasses.

This is how we eventually shoot it at "magic hour," that special time poised between day and night — *entre chien et loup,* as the romantic French call it, when you can't distinguish between dog and wolf. The scene, where we taunt the Deity, is a little over the top — I feel like Lear railing against the storm. We get it in two takes; the reverses will be done in Bracciano, providing a chance to embellish — or at least tone it all down. Then, I suggest, we should be filmed with our faces bloodily incarnadined by the cascading wine, but Brian's already thought of the same thing — in slow motion!

High drama is exchanged for real-life drama when, back at the hotel, the TV reports the overthrow in Yugoslavia of another media-manipulating tyrant, Slobodan Milosevic.

FRIDAY, OCTOBER 6TH

We film our own dictator scene outside one of the most famous and imposing buildings in the world. In my baggage I have a description of it in Charles Dickens' *Pictures of Italy*, a text I'm due to record the moment I return to LA. "It is the most impressive, the most stately, the most solemn, grand, majestic, mournful sight, conceivable. Never, in its bloodiest prime, can the sight of the Coliseum, full and running over with the lustiest life, have moved one's heart, as it must move all who look upon it now, a ruin God be thanked: a ruin!" There's no Ridley Scott computer wizardry now — it's so real it overwhelms, rising to the sky like a great stone tsunami.

The air is humid and clouds gather menacingly over the massive edifice. I think of all the other great Roman monuments I have been lucky enough to use as film sets — the Pantheon and the "Wedding Cake" Vittorio Emmanuele Monument whose marble interior was as frigid as the white stone exterior of fascist EUR. I first stayed here helping to tame *The Shrew,* and it was also here that Julie Taymor so effectively created the Rome of her Titus Andronicus.

The benefits of thoroughly learning the scene pay off as the set, jammed with tourists, has a Roman holiday, carnival atmosphere. The distractions are incessant — at one point someone strolls through the shot jabbering on a cell phone! I wander off and find a quiet corner to concentrate.

I'm delighted to see Diane included in the scene, especially when she again serves soothing tea — even producing a china teapot with delicate porcelain cups. With her jet-black hair, discreet jewelry, and elegant dress, she looks the perfect hostess.

Complimented by Pat on her Gertrude in the Ethan Hawke *Hamlet,* Diane tells an interesting story that perfectly illustrates the improvisatory nature of so much filmmaking. Arriving on the New York location on the very first morning, she found that the shoes provided were far too big. Even stuffed with paper they made her totter, prompting the instant decision to play her Gertrude as a drunk, with an inebriate stagger.

The set is finally ready and the scene goes well. In this Roman context I feel kinship with Silvio Berlusconi, the local media mogul who, emulating Alexander, is now making that fateful transition to politics. My speech is even cheered to the echo by the tourists, who have been co-opted as extras. There's also a reaction — whether of approbation or otherwise is unclear — from the heavens as thunder rumbles. I'm reminded of Lenin's definition of the movies: "History written in lightning."

My work is finished by lunchtime, and Pat and I leave the set, where more scenes with Noah and Elisa will be filmed, including a first kiss. There will also be a scene of people running in panic from the Colosseum that will later be integrated with a shot of a model of the building collapsing. We return to the Trattoria Othello where, just as Romeo courted his Juliet at a feast, so I once romanced my Pat from languid lunch to leisurely dinner. Sitting again by the gurgling fountain piled with fresh fruits and vegetables, we enjoy the memories as much as the meal.

Back at the hotel, we revise our travel plans for Ghent. I determine to emulate Udo, who has already jetted off yet again, and whiz from capital to capital. I continue my search for suitable Shakespeare quotes for Noah, to dovetail our personalities. It's now raining hard and I think of the crew getting drenched. Although uncomfortable to work in, the downpour shouldn't hold us up; unless backlit, it won't show up on film.

In a break in the deluge I go shopping with Pat, but loathe the noisy, shoving, umbrella'd, car-dodging confines of the Via del Corso, as chaotically crowded as in Dickens' day. Pat wants me to buy clothes for myself, but I'm not in the mood (I rarely am!), even though I'm surrounded by articles of near-irresistible desirability. There's a damp red sky at night promising, I hope, fairer weather to filmmaker as well as shepherd. Certainly nothing is more dismal than Bracciano, where we're heading tomorrow, in the rain.

At dinner with Matt and Brian, I learn that, miraculously, the rain held off on the set, apart from a few sprinkles at lunchtime. Perhaps, after all, the gods were thundering the celestial equivalent of the thumbs-up. Further divine providence is revealed behind Matt's decision not to film in Israel, apart from a second unit sent to record staged scenes of people fleeing in chaos — the exact same scenes now being played out for real on the nightly news.

Another TV story featured is Slobo's devilish political

maneuver, congratulating his victorious opponent while announcing his own imminent return to political life. Will he get away with it? Or will he fall like the overreaching Alexander, and hang in the main square of a Belgrade battered and degraded by his epic duplicity?

Brian reveals that his father is a war hero and we discuss a similar historical revisionism in contemporary movies, where the heroic deeds of his father's generation are blithely transferred to other nationalities. Americans retrieve and decode the "Enigma" machine, while the British are portrayed as sadistic mass murderers, worthy of Slobo's highest military honors.

Noah joins us in our suite and, comparing notes, we discuss further our shared character. After passing on points discovered in both films, I tell him how I admired his courage in virtually going from the plane to the set, and acting an intimate scene with Elisa within hours of meeting her. Screen passion, however, is usually more technical than erotic, often played to an audience of yawning grips. And Noah is a seasoned pro — he's been acting since he was fourteen, and now stands on the brink of great things.

He's conscientious, too, rushing off to a violin lesson — even after having practiced till 1:00 this morning!

SATURDAY, OCTOBER 7TH

There's more drama at breakfast with a crew member who is obviously having some kind of breakdown. I listen in genuine sympathy, making it my duty to ensure that all our other producers are aware. Much as I empathize with the suffering involved, however, it's a brutal case of shape up or ship out. The production simply cannot afford to hemorrhage vitality from any part of its complex body.

We pack, amazed that luggage can breed so fast and produce so much stuff, while the Scientology convention jazz band serenades us lustily from the Corso below. Is this another of L. Ron Hubbard's insidious tests — to discover the human aural breaking point? It makes me wonder if the film of his, *Battlefield Earth,* faith-based like ours but boasting a bigger budget and starring John Travolta, will be equally noisily promoted.

The streets are crowded to the point that rats, in the same density, would go mad in their cages. Hell, in this case, is indeed other people. We have been invited to lunch with Franco Zeffirelli in his villa on the Appia Antica. Even our driver, Alessandro, is exasperated with the millennial mobs, estimated at some thirty million visitors for the year.

The clotted traffic slows us to walking speed along the ancient cobbled street. I think wistfully of my *Austin Powers* director, Jay Roach, who told me he sped to work on a skateboard in an equally traffic-jammed New York! We eventually pass the villa we once rented on another movie. It came with its own vineyard providing ambrosial libations, but insufficient, it seemed, to assuage the wrath of another former tenant, Frank Sinatra. Dissatisfied with the amenities provided, he had apparently flushed the bath towels down the toilet, inflicting damage to the system that we paid for daily.

Franco's present villa is close to the one we stayed in as his guests during the filming of *Romeo and Juliet*. Always lively and full of interesting people, it was vibrant with the images of heat and light that Shakespeare's words so potently evoked, and it seemed to forever echo with laughter and music. Now it looks cold and dark in the driving rain.

The Maestro is seated at his huge worktable, busily designing — and, as we find out, making up for lost time. He can barely rise to greet us and proceeds to tell a chilling story of torture worthy of the Borgias. Apparently an operation to repair a failing hip replacement had gone disastrously wrong, suffusing his whole body with a horrible infection that still obliges him to live with a permanent infusion of antibiotics. It was only the promised delivery of several important commissions for next year's Verdi centennial that had kept him from succumbing, like his teenage Romeo and Juliet, to the Old Apothecary's "mortal drugs."

Even if his body has been slowed down, Franco's spirit is as vivacious as ever and the old mischievous humor still flashes in his pale blue eyes. We eat, as in days gone by, encircling him round the table. Vige, his cook, produces her same succulent pasta, which is served by Dorino the butler, now as gray-haired as his master. Even Franco's cherished Jack Russells no longer seem quite so sprightly.

I'm so glad to see him after all these years. With my own hip operation a success, my heart goes out to him. We exchange books — my Shakespeare tome for an exquisite volume of his stage designs. The rain thunders down outside like the artificial deluge he created on the set of the The Shrew for my arrival as Lucentio in Padua. Nothing then could dampen my excitement at entering the wondrous new realm of cinema. Franco opened the gates of the city for me and, for that, I shall always be grateful

After lunch, photographs and fond farewells, we speed northward to Bracciano and back to the Hotel Alfredo. We even have our old room, 310, a sort of suite with a pair of minuscule bathrooms and two matching balconies overlooking the lake. After a week on the road, it feels good to fully unpack.

Going for a walk along the lakeside, there are the same swans fighting over food and lovers canoodling inside steamed up cars. At dinner we enjoy the same local specialty, risotto with nettles, served by the same waiter who, coincidentally, once worked in a LA restaurant not far from our house. The sameness of it all, the sense of continuity, is reassuring. It was also comforting to notice, when we arrived, the same auspicious rainbow arching over the lake to welcome us back.

CHAPTER SEVEN

Foreign Campaigns

SUNDAY, OCTOBER 8TH

Awaking at dawn to an extravagant technicolor sunrise, I race for my camera. By the time I'm ready, however, it has faded away like an old photograph: "Heard melodies are sweet, but those unheard are sweeter," I reassure myself. Breakfast is not the same without last year's goddess of a waitress. We learn that she's now married and pregnant — again, a question of seizing that photographic moment!

It's a beautiful autumn morning — sunny, crisp, and fresh after the rain. The lake, according to the approximate English of the guide issued by our helpful Italian co-producers, "occupying the crateriche cavities of the Sabatini volcanos," is a cool, cobalt blue.

At the foot of the castle's "pentagonal plant with poderose cylindrical towers," we discover Diane with Gil Colon (who plays Colonel Rick Howard, David Alexander's loyal lieutenant) picking their way through the Sunday flea market. Diane has purchased antique china, but our bargains are more practical: perfumed candles and aromatherapy oils for the room to mask the post-summer perfume from the drains in the loos.

In town nothing has changed. Why should it? It has slept for hundreds of years and nothing seems to have awakened it since our last visit. The narrow streets, made for horse and carriage, are still crammed with anachronistic cars; the bells continue to toll from the sixteenth-century tower of St. Stephen's church.

Walking down the hill to the lakeshore, we pass hedgerows brimming with berries and wild cyclamen. Our timing is perfect: We are seated in the Golden Pike restaurant an instant before it is flooded with families in their Sunday best, with grandmothers bouncing babies, old men in waistcoats and hats, be-jeaned young couples and noisy boys, all celebrating like extras in an Italian comedy.

We saunter back beside the quiet lake. It's very much out of season: Most stores are boarded up and the holiday steamer rides at anchor, waiting out the winter. All this peace is in tremendous contrast to the nonstop brouhaha in Rome, a world away down the Via Cassia.

Lulled by the unwonted tranquility, we soon drowse over books and script. Pat, after preparing two photographic shows in a row, must be wound as tight as the film in her camera. She can now relax: The success of both of them has been confirmed in recent reviews.

I make post-siesta tea with my portable plastic kettle — instant room service. It's one of my most treasured possessions, along with the telescopic luggage trolley that serves as an instant porter anywhere. Both make travel almost tolerable. Certainly my kettle is protection against that witches' brew served up as "tea" in coffee-obsessed America, made in a pot that has already played host to the bean with its pungent, ineradicable smell.

In the late afternoon, we take another stroll by the now

golden lake. I see Gil rowing in the distance, while Brian swims. I have no urge to join him. I remember once filming in the Caribbean in a similar idyllic spot and plunging ecstatically into a local river — only to discover later that it was a notorious breeding ground for bilharzia, a parasitic disease that only a Stone Alexander could love. Instead we watch the swans being fed by a sunlit child in a white confirmation dress who looks as though she might just float off with them.

But then the fairy tale fades; in the evening, I start to shiver and my throat is sore. Damn! — the first fluey symptoms. Acting while ill is always a challenge as, unlike most jobs, time off is not encouraged. The show, as they say, must go on. I recall filming an entire fight in *The Three Musketeers* while my guts were being cut and thrust internally by some gastric villain. But my friend, Derek Jacobi, reported even worse horrors while playing Shakespeare in some developing country: The cast was so ill that diapers had to be worn and buckets strategically placed in the wings!

At an early dinner, I encounter Brian and we discuss one of the last scenes we're to film. It's where I insult the portrait of Christ and exult about my impending victory. The script has me hurling wine at the painting, but now that seems overdone after the powerful scene we've already filmed on the ramparts with Udo where wine was liberally and graphically employed. Brian agrees to my suggestion of a much more low-key approach, very quiet and menacing, with Stone reading some heretical text by a flickering fire — finally wearing that monkish cowl that we conceived of so long ago. I notice that our troubled crew member is still dining with us. Preferring continuity to conflict, I'm very glad.

Pat falls asleep early; I know I should pick up our LA phone calls, but soon it's. . . .

MONDAY, OCTOBER 9TH

I feel better; homeopathy has exerted its usual subtle healing — or was it the aromatherapy? The assistant director has let me "stand by" at the hotel, rather than be herded onto the set in the usual "hurry up and wait" mode. All those neglected phone calls, faxes, and messages are now dispatched. By lunchtime I still haven't been called, and Pat

and I repair anew to the Golden Pike. It's now deserted —
a pale, silent shadow of its Sunday best. Given a table by
the scenic window, we order the same delicious *corregone*
lake fish, though tempted by the house cannelloni that the
menu describes as "stuffed rools of noodie dough"!

I'm reminded of menu mayhem elsewhere: "Ladies are
requested not to have children in the bar" in Norway, and
the Mexican "The manager has personally passed all the
water served here." Even the correct Swiss are not immune:
"Our wines leave you nothing to hope for." Certainly yesterday's mobbed meal brings to mind a notice spotted elsewhere in Italy: "This hotel is renowned for its peace and
solitude. In fact, crowds from all over the world flock here
to enjoy its solitude."

In the afternoon, I re-enter both castle and movie. Just
walking up the long, steep path from the courtyard to the
castle is a keep-fit workout in itself. But this is nothing compared to the physical challenge facing the grips who, in addition, have to maneuver the heavy equipment. Using a
medieval rope and tackle, they haul cameras and lights up
the precipitous "poderose" walls and into the towering struc-

ture through an upper window. How Stone loves being on top of his world!

We film on the herringbone-pattern staircase where we shot the first scene here of *The Omega Code*. Yet again, a pleasing synchronicity. Now I'm returning from Africa and my world tour, and they've found a beautiful chauffeur-driven Bentley to convey Udo and myself in style. I feel charged with combative energy as I encounter Gabriella, awaiting me. Diane plays it very simply and physically — collapsing in an unhappy heap on the steps as I bound up them. The scene is completed, ensuring that I'm now free to return with Pat to Ghent tomorrow.

Diane and I agree to work that evening with John Fasano on the remaining dialogue for our still underdeveloped scenes. Over dinner, we conclude that what is missing is a sort of love scene — an expression of the sensual tie that still binds them before Gabriella discovers her husband's true identity. The new "violin scene" on the battlements, after the triumphant Colosseum speech, is deemed to be the ideal place for this.

Packing (again!) and early to bed (again!).

TUESDAY, OCTOBER 10TH

Up early (again!) to witness several Megiddans practicing Tai Chi under Gil's supervision in the twilight. I feel less frivolous about leaving when I encounter Michael Biehn, also setting out on his grand tour of Italy. What a treat lies ahead: As Dr. Samuel Johnson remarked, with a pertinence undiminished by time, "A man who has not been in Italy is always conscious of an inferiority." Pat and I suggest several "musts," more culinary than cultural, such as a Bellini cocktail at Harry's Bar in Venice.

I notice Rob Bredow setting off too, going native on a Vespa with his sweet wife perched behind him. This other, more benign "wasp" was my mode of travel as a young actor at Dundee Rep in Scotland, where even the highlands were no barrier to this exhilarating two-wheeled transport.

Breakfast with Diane and John where we continue last night's discussions. John promises to fax a draft outline to Ghent — and it's there in the Sofitel when Pat and I check in again later that afternoon. I like it; it's both sexy and menacing, and I fax back my approval.

One of the highlights of the film festival is tonight's

concert to be given by Hans Zimmer, the prolific and successful film composer. Musicians and singers are flying in from all over the world to accompany him and pay homage. Hans' elegant mother joins us for tea, guiltily off-loading her own accumulated hoard of chocolates. But the most delicious luxury is a hot bath, a simple but soul-satisfying pleasure after so many trickly showers.

Then, off to the concert in a file of limousines with police escort and flashing lights, like Soviet politicians barreling down the center of the road to the Kremlin. The show is staged in a vast velodrome, recalling the Taormina festival where films are projected in the Graeco-Roman theater. The whole soirée proves immensely enjoyable. Lisa Gerrard, whose ethereal voice haunts the sound track of *Gladiator*, elicits unanimous approval. Hans, who has never before performed his music in public, also triumphs.

Supper is at midnight — a huge cornucopia of goodies piled in profusion like the seafood and fruit in Flemish old master paintings. Another unforgettable film festival feast comes to mind — in Kazakstan. On the wide steppe outside Almaty, Pat and I were entertained in a yurt, a capacious round felt tent. As the guest from Hollywood, I was honored with the greatest delicacy, a sheep's eye washed down with fermented mare's milk. Fortunately, with all human eyes on me, I managed to secretly substitute my prize for some nuts, thus disgracing neither my own nor my hosts' national honor, by being seen to munch and swallow with a gusto that only long training in the actor's art could simulate!

Bed at 2:00 AM — bang goes that monastic Bracciano regime!

WEDNESDAY, OCTOBER 11TH

Breakfast with Régis Wargnier at the Sofitel, in a room lined with movie star portraits. The talented film director of *Indochine* and other multicultural films, Régis met us at the Sochi film festival by the Black Sea a few years ago. This event, rumored to be run by a Russian mafioso, lacked for nothing. The ultimate treat was having a casual, *al fresco* lunch amidst the ghosts of formal uniforms and long white muslin frocks in Czar Nicholas' former hunting lodge, which our host was transforming into an hotel.

Now we are joined by Lisa Gerrard, impeccably groomed in her signature structured clothes like a fantasy antipodean version of Gabriella. There is instant rapport: Pat takes her to St. Peter's Abbey to see her exhibition and she's there an hour later, enchanted. At one point Lisa breaks into an impromptu aria and I respond with a Shakespearean oration, the mingled sounds reverberating up into the lofty ceiling amidst the fading echoes of generations of ecclesiastical music.

We lunch in the crypt with other guests participating in an official seminar on music in film. After last night's roof-rousing success, when the cinema's usual servant became its undeniable star, the importance of a film's score cannot be denied — although Lisa confides that Ridley Scott was made to choose between having another expensive "arty" shot in the film, or using her in its sound track. It's quite apparent he made the correct decision. Lisa seems very calm and centered — just as well as she faces an interminable flight back to Melbourne this afternoon.

Back at the hotel we run into Hans and his beautiful wife Suzy who, apparently, only got to bed at 5:00 this morning! We all retire to the bar for yet more tea (and chocolates). Hans is a curious and beguiling mixture of English public school, German aesthete, and American show-business. We know him slightly from parties in LA. Any attempts to get to know him better are hijacked by the relentlessly cheerful hotel manager who insists on posing us for photographs. There's polite acquiescence — the hotel is, after all, a festival sponsor — but my wife is as direct as ever. "Could we have some peace, please?" she sweetly asks. And we get it.

Rushing off to be tourists, we first view the famous Van Eyk altarpiece, *The Adoration of the Lamb*, in St. Bavo's Cathedral. It is stunningly beautiful, with a big, healthy blonde girl, like our very own Bracciano Madonna, as the Virgin. Commissioned by a local cloth merchant, the clothing and draperies are lovingly detailed — it's like looking at a medieval fashion magazine. One panel is a copy of the stolen original. Apparently on his deathbed, the thief tried to confess as to its whereabouts and had just managed to whisper, "It's at. . . " when he expired! There's recorded music playing in the church — something that every empty, echoing ecclesiastical building should emulate.

We next take a trip on the River Leie, drifting past the facades of gothic guild houses, and the occasional baroque intrusion. It's intimate, accessible and very relaxing — more laid-back San Antonio than hyperactive Venice.

After so much pleasure, I make a quick, slightly guilty phone call to our production office to see that all's well. It is — although I learn that the schedule has now grown by a day, making that planned upstate New York visit impossible.

Off to the official festival opening. Morgan Freeman's in the lobby looking a little frayed but still smiling after a day of interviews and, no doubt, the gracious iteration *ad nauseam* of the same words. We encounter other LA friends, Mace Neufeld and his girlfriend Diane. Mace is on the jury — hard but enjoyable work if the movies are good, as they were in Gerardmer, but maddening if otherwise. Bad ones, though, are instructive as to what constitutes a good movie, which, because it *is* good, is essentially *trompe l'oeil* and impossible to analyze.

The opening Gala certainly has a great film: Julie Taymor's *Titus,* which restores Shakespeare's play to the significance — and box office success — that it enjoyed in Elizabethan times. We've already seen and loved it, so we accept an invitation to dine with other guests at a delightful country restaurant.

I find myself sitting next to Julie and her musician husband, Elliot Goldenthal, who has himself created many superb film scores, including the one for *Titus.* Julie and I talk about the time, almost twenty years ago, that we worked together on a Broadway stage musical based on *The Little Prince* in which I played a St. Exupéry–style airman. Julie was both set and costume designer, and she was fired — for having too many ideas! Without her imaginative contribution, the production crashed like the aviator's stricken plane in the Sahara.

Julie had taken Pat to see an off-Broadway show that highlighted her designing genius, with its extraordinary amalgam of visual and cultural influences that would later set the Lion King so triumphantly roaring. Over dinner Julie, ebullient and brilliant as ever, tells me about her aborted plans for *The Little Prince:* the little model planes that the dancers were to hold aloft, for example, so that they filled the stage sky with flight. I'm sick with a momentary regret . . .

THURSDAY, OCTOBER 12TH

Pat is staying on an extra day for further PR work on her exhibition, so I return alone to the Brussels airport under cloud-flecked Flemish skies. This time it's the baggage handlers who are on strike, whereupon my priceless porter springs instantly into action, toting my bag to the gate — where (surprise!?), I discover the flight is delayed "due to the late arrival of the crew"!

Hans' mother arrives, elegant and coiffed despite the early hour, and we chat like old friends. She's heading home to Munich, the setting for so many of my favorite film experiences, including Hal Prince's *Something for Everyone,* Bob Fosse's *Cabaret* and Billy Wilder's *Fedora.* Munich, the city where Hitler came to power, also represents the twin poles of the German genius, with grim Dachau cheek by jowl with rococo Nymphenburg. I have always enjoyed filming in Germany, from the fog-bound fastness of its Baltic coast to the forests and castles of Bavaria.

Mrs. Zimmer's Lufthansa flight departs with teutonic punctuality, reminding me of the time when the airline defied its schedule and, putting humanity before efficiency, mercifully waited for us at the Moscow airport. Pat and I had been standing in an interminable line at the passport control while our flight's final call was announced. We were about to be processed when Pat was shoved aside by a self-important mafioso type. Erupting like an October revolution, she hurled this man's passport the length of the departure hall while at the same time lecturing the astonished bystanders not to put up with such rudeness. Having expected to spend the night in jail, I was more than relieved when we were hustled to the waiting plane that raced for the runway the second we stepped gratefully inside.

I find a seat to wait and, despite a Siberia of empty chairs, someone sits down right next to me. I'm too bored to move; besides, I persuade myself that this is the raw material of my job, observing my fellow creatures at first hand and not from the isolated distance of a VIP lounge.

The flight is eventually called, and I'm hauling my suitcase onto the bus just as someone asks me to pose for a photo. This is the equivalent of the cruel practice of being photographed after arriving on an overnight flight. I smile — and am rewarded on the plane with a favorite window seat and no involuntary travelling companion. The sense of relief at finally departing is nothing compared to that formerly experienced flying out of Communist countries when one's passport was continually checked by armed and suspicious soldiers all the way to the plane door.

There are spectacular views en route to the Alps where clouds gather, and we bump and grind our way through a white nothingness that lulls me into a reverie about other memorable flights to Rome. There was that life-changing one where I travelled down from London with other hopefuls to audition for Lucentio in Zeffirelli's *Shrew:* "For I have Pisa left / And am to Padua come, as he that leaves / A shallow plash to plunge him in the deep, / And with satiety seeks to quench his thirst."

Later, as an established film actor, "in the deep" and travelling to meet on a film concerning a defecting Russian ballet dancer (then a popular and recurring theme), I was entertained by the stewardess to some of the pleasures of *la dolce vita* in a totally empty first-class cabin. I remember pre-Pat, before stewardesses were unsexed into flight attendants, a blonde Pan American with whom I once dined, and no doubt wined, in Rome. Years later she served me dinner on some flight, the intervening years and miles having transformed us both, for "Time doth transfix the flourish set on youth, / And delves the parallels in beauty's brow."

I'm aroused from all this remembrance of things past as land focuses into view again: "I am arriv'd for fruitful Lombardy, / The pleasant garden of great Italy." The words are as fresh and unforgettable today as they were all those years ago. Coming in to land, the plane banks directly over Bracciano and my castle, as if welcoming me back. Alessandro awaits me too and we speed back to the location. I've been called in for a violin lesson, confirming that the scene is now officially part of the new schedule. Bravo! Bravissimo!

After greeting my fellow Megiddans and distributing the

inevitable chocolate gifts, I get down to work with my youthful instructor, Luigi, all in fulfillment of that other Shakespearean observation, "the Devil rides upon a fiddlestick." I don't feel quite as dedicated as Noah, assuming that the elaborate fingering of the Paganini piece can be faked.

In general I enjoy mastering all the eclectic skills that an actor is required to acquire, such as riding, fencing, driving, sailing, flying — even walking the circus high wire. But I especially enjoy playing music, once relishing the power of conducting the Orchestre de Grenoble in a movement from Haydn's *Military Symphony,* learned by rote. And I still have the residue of the callous grooved into my finger, indispensable for playing the sitar in Merchant-Ivory's romantic 1960's film, *The Guru.*

The session goes well and I'm about to leave when one of the Italian crew takes me aside, mentioning that I should never have worn my purple T-shirt on the set. The color is bad luck — just as chrysanthemums are here. Fellini would have banished me in a trice, no doubt in a flurry of touched testicles and other Italian folklore to ward off the evil eye. Suitably chastened, I apologize profusely.

One has to be so careful! A black cat is, for the English, a symbol of good fortune, whereas for the Irish, it's a sign of the Devil! In the theater — in England at least — the sight of a black cat at a rehearsal presages success, and the exact opposite during a performance.

Is it just that actors are more superstitious than other mortals? I think of the elaborate ritual requested of any miscreant found whistling in a dressing room to exorcise its ill effects; and everyone knows the opprobrium attached to anyone wilfully quoting Shakespeare's "Scottish Play" inside a theater. I remember, too, that when two former actors, President and Mrs. Reagan, retired from the White House to an LA house, they refused to move in until its street number had been changed from 666 — the mark of the Beast!

Back at the hotel I run into Udo, who plies me with a local sticky pastry and equally delicious gossip, promising to tell me all that has transpired in my brief absence. Perhaps his Guardian is really a close relation of Farfarello, Dante's scandal-mongering demon in *The Divine Comedy!*

I telephone Pat as, outside, a huge moon emerges from the lake like a yellow balloon and climbs into the still, starry sky. Both to get some air and to enjoy the spectacle, I walk to the restaurant. Garbo-like, I wish to be alone after so much intense socializing, not least to study the scene for tomorrow. I stroll back in the moonlight, round the lake that now gleams like a silver tea tray, reflecting on how blessed I am to lead this charmed life.

CHAPTER EIGHT

New Fronts

FRIDAY, OCTOBER 13TH

The self-satisfied reflections of the previous evening are cut short this Friday the 13th, which lives up to its dire reputation. Today is finally when we are to shoot "The Scene" that has been postponed from the very start of filming. In it, Gabriella is provoked into slapping Alexander; but in rehearsal, Diane misjudges the distances and hits me hard. Momentarily disoriented, my head pounds while my eye starts to blacken — punishment, no doubt, for wearing that purple T-shirt. I retire to the makeup room and dose myself liberally with the crew's Belgian chocolates.

Brian wants to simplify the scene — and I need to do something active while Diane has her long speech — but without involving us in complex and time-consuming moves. I decide to pour myself a glass of brandy as I listen. (Shakespeare always focuses speeches on inanimate objects like suns, moons, and daggers — and actors never know what to do with their hands!).

It works. I can sit down, too, with Diane at my feet — and even hurl the glass into the fireplace, an action that speaks much louder than any words. There's another fatal contact: This time a kiss of death with Diane. I improvise a "good-bye" as Stone, already the Beast in human form, ruptures what's left of their relationship. The scene feels charged and dramatic.

Afterward I report for a violin lesson, but the instrument seems too difficult to hold with my head still discordantly throbbing *molto agitato*. Cutting the session short, I get a massage from a local girl, but this proves to be equally punishing. I'm reminded of a time in the early 70s when, stricken with flu just before the Broadway world premiere of Tennessee Williams' *Outcry*, I was treated by a shiatsu masseur found by Pat. Like sushi, shiatsu was then relatively unknown and I thought she had played a horrible trick as I outcried in agony at every vicious prod. But it enabled me to perform with extraordinary energy and focus.

I have rented a car and it's there in the castle yard awaiting me: a gleaming Renault Scénic. But it's impenetrably blocked in by trucks, vans, and other cars; all my driving skills are thoroughly exercised under the critical — dare I say, challenging — eyes of the production drivers encircling me. This is not the day for reckless travel! The car lives up to its name as it carefully rounds the now-familiar bend in the road to reveal a panorama of blue lake, green fields, and pastel distant mountains.

I relish this renewed four-wheeled freedom, one that has enabled Pat and me to explore the world together. It has not been without its adventures. There was the time our car overheated in the Sahara and had to be topped up with bottled water more expensive than gasoline. On another occasion, we slid off an icy mountain road outside Belgrade. A helpful stranger came to our rescue, claiming to know how to drive us out of these difficult conditions. Once behind the wheel, however, he swept off with car — and wife — like a bandit of old, leaving me to hitchhike back to the city where, thankfully, I found both delivered, and intact.

There's another reunion with Pat, who has her own Friday the 13th horror story. Her flight down from Brussels was so bad that she requested a complaint form from the laconic attendant, only to be told that this would be pointless as *everyone* complained! All this must be especially galling for Pat who, as travel editor of *Glamour*, once sampled a pampered world from a permanent first-class seat.

That evening I drive Pat, John Fasano, and Gary Bettman — still trailing rolls of faxes like a comic Roman actor — to dinner at a distant lakeshore restaurant. As well as reviewing our progress, we discuss accidents on sets and the responsibilities involved. I recall Régis Wargnier telling me that, while filming *East-West* in Bulgaria his star, Sandrine Bonnaire, had to be sent back to France for treatment after a mishap with a slap on the set. I once broke an actor's nose in the course of a night-shot fight. But instead of retaliating, he thanked me profusely as, for the first time, he was now able to breathe freely! The phrase, "there, but for the grace of God. . . ," however, has especial significance for me, having witnessed the ultimate horror, the death of a colleague while filming a riding shot.

On a lighter note, we discover — far too late, for he is leaving us tomorrow — that John has a gift for imitating us all, especially me! He is also obsessed by insects that he claims are filling his room. Perhaps this phobia is the real genesis of the wasp scene. They could be coming from David Hedison's room, I suggest, as David — then known as Al — created much "buzz" in 1958's *The Fly* alongside that consummate ghoul-meister, Vincent Price.

SATURDAY, OCTOBER 14TH

Up with the blind-piercing sun. At breakfast, people are already behaving territorially, occupying their "own" tables. I notice Stephan sitting with his wife, Jennifer, who is taking a brief break from that supremely demanding role, playing

Mom. They both wear identical, spikey hairdos as if their quiet conversation is somehow shocking! Perhaps Stephan is telling her about his new role as an actor, playing one of my guardsmen. I wonder if Matt will essay a role too?

I chat with Gavin, my mini-me, who has the most exquisitely expressive eyes — and, thank goodness, doesn't seem aware of this. He's off to use them sightseeing in Rome with his nice mother. Lucky kid: He's only eight. What *will* he think? What must it be like to be a child actor, to live so much of the time in a fantasy world, dealing with those "two impostors, Triumph and Disaster" at an abnormally early age?

But Gavin seems the quintessence of normality as he plays with Cody and Caylan, Matt and Laurie's boys. It's interesting to see them fixated for hours on their Game-Boy gizmos. Whatever happened to good old-fashioned books? Gavin explains his Super Mario game to Pat who, now heavily into photography of the brain, compliments it for building dendrites!

The charming Franco Nero, who plays General Francini, Gabriella's father, has invited us to a movie premiere in

Rome tomorrow night and I telephone him to arrange a meeting place. He tells Pat how much he and Vanessa Redgrave enjoyed her exhibition at the Moscow Film Festival, the last time we all met. My next call is to my parents in England as the newspapers headline the devastating floods there, particularly in Lewes, Sussex, where they live. My mother reports from the water-logged front. It's like an outtake from our movie — huge storms, collapsing buildings, and no trains.

Brian surfaces at his door with a heavy cold — so much for swimming in the lake! We're off to the big city, Bracciano, to buy the *Herald Tribune* as well as guidebooks and maps for tourist jaunts. The little town has surprisingly sophisticated shopping. Last year Pat bought the sexiest lingerie at an unassuming little store that, from the outside, looked as though it only dealt in ancient corsets and beige knitwear. She also walked away with some equally seductive sneakers that are the envy of LA.

Afterward we drive out, up and over the crest of the encircling ancient volcano and down toward the coast, past fields of blonde, horned cattle standing still like furry statues. At San Marinella there's fresh sea air, even fresher grilled fish, and a walk on the long sandy beach. Then to Cerveteri to see the world-famous Etruscan tombs.

We arrive just as the necropolis is closing but — the upside to being recognized — are given a personal tour by three of the guides as they make their final inspection round for the night. The price of admission is a group photograph. In its now-deserted setting and the fading light, this sepulchral, stone city looks extraordinary. Architectural styles are varied — some tombs are even more spacious than our hotel room, but with equally hard beds. We have the place to ourselves, apart from the ghosts enjoying the good life of the afterlife. I mention to one of the ladies that I'm filming with Franco Nero, and she goes weak at the knees. Perhaps I can send her his photo, too!

Later that evening, I practice my violin, but with Pat in the room, feel somewhat inhibited. I bear in mind that definition of a gentleman as "someone who knows how to play the bagpipes but refrains from doing so." At dusk we go for supper in medieval Aguilera, perched on a rocky spur just round the lake. Mammoth pizzas are served by a

Swedish girl who says she has been here six years having "found my paradise." Her swarthy Adam regards his blonde Eve proprietorially from the flaming oven.

SUNDAY, OCTOBER 15TH

Pouring rain! We loiter indoors and I talk to Matt about our film. We discuss future plans — even the possibility of an *Omega Code 3*. It's plausible: He shows me the Bible passage in "Revelation," Chapter 20, where the Devil returns to the world again. "And he (the Angel) laid hold on the Dragon, that old serpent, which is the Devil, and Satan, and bound him a thousand years and cast him into the bottomless pit, and shut him up, and set a seal upon him, that he should deceive the nations no more, till the thousand years should be fulfilled: *and after that he must be loosed a little season.*"

Matt confides that he and Stephan Blinn are also working on a "bible" for a possible *Omega* TV series. Would I be interested in being involved? Of course I am — how could I conceive of Stone Alexander being played by someone else!

I'm invited to view the dailies — or weeklies, in our case — on an Avid machine in the hotel basement, which seems to have been transformed into the local entertainment center; there's even a ballroom dancing class on some evenings. The footage, especially the cut sequences, impresses even in this squashed-down ratio. Our conversations have a special resonance — it's exactly a year ago, to the day, that *The Omega Code* was released.

That evening Pat and I decide not to brave the wet drive to Rome, with its unfamiliar streets and impossible parking, for the film premier. Everything there begins and ends far too late — we both much prefer the simpler pleasures of our little cell, even though the dim, blue lighting suggests activities more appropriate to the boudoir than the study.

While I watch the BBC World Service through a blizzard of static, Pat sets about arranging a dinner party in LA for John Major — he'll be lecturing there on our return. She telephones to invite Steve Martin, an old and valued friend, who reveals that his book *Shopgirl* is now number one on the *LA Times* book list. I wonder how much of it he wrote in rooms like ours, as he did his play, *Picasso at the Lapin Agile,* created largely while hotel-bound in Australia.

Certainly Harold Pinter must have written *The Birthday Party* while still an actor lodging in "digs," as their atmosphere of suffocating respectability is so perfectly captured. And Pat penned much of her screenplay while marooned in a Florida hotel on location with me. Such reflections on the creative forces unleashed by alien abodes make me even more content to remain "home," rather than roam a rainy and frivolous Rome.

MONDAY, OCTOBER 16TH

Up early to gray skies. The TV carries pictures of the even angrier skies in northern Italy where torrential rain has provoked monstrous floods. The whole world seems to be auditioning for this movie! All this meteorological mayhem discourages Pat's plan to fly to Milan to meet up with an old friend, Giorgio Armani, whose incomparable clothes we, and Stone Alexander, so admire.

Other TV footage shows disaster averted: Kostunica, the new leader in Serbia, is holding firm against Slobo's machinations, heeding Edmund Burke's warning that "All that is needed for the triumph of evil is for good men to do nothing." Perhaps the old tyrant will now share the Beast's fate and be sent down to where he belongs.

I'm not working as the scenes being filmed are with Noah. He's engaged in a "paint battle" with fellow cadets, where the strategic ruthlessness that defines our shared role will make a literal and lethal splash. Pat and I head off down memory lane to Tuscania and revisit San Pietro, the church where, thirty-four years ago, the Zeffirelli *Romeo and Juliet* was filmed.

The town is first glimpsed perched picturesquely around medieval towers on a high hill. The church, overlooking a lovely valley and dating back to the eleventh century, enchants with its carved stonework, columns, and magnificent rose window. Inside, an old lady selling postcards reminisces about the filming, pointing out the inlaid marble floor, polished by the centuries to worn smoothness, where our young lovers were betrothed.

Next door there's a trattoria serving technicolor-fresh salads as well as sensational pane cotta. Pat has developed a disturbing addiction, as strong as her passion for tapioca pudding, to this delicious dessert, ingesting one at nearly every meal. Our new car is proving to be a simple joy to drive and, camel-like, seems to go forever between liquid refills. My only complaint is that in the land of Verdi and Rossini, its radio plays nothing but idiotic Europop.

Back in Bracciano there's treasure trove: an English *Sunday Times* with the latest news of Britain's dysfunctional royal family — and of my Corfu dancing partner who one day might be Queen. The present Queen is coming soon to Rome. As both Her Majesty and the Pope are heads of their respective churches, who gives the audience to whom, I wonder.

The newspaper's horoscope orders me and my fellow Aries to accomplish everything in the next few days before a Mercury retrograde bogs things down. This prompts a flurry of faxes and phone calls, and I send the promised photos to our Three Graces of the necropolis. We respond to the mail FedExed from home, but at this distance, most of it seems irrelevant.

THURSDAY, OCTOBER 17TH

Breakfasting with Brian and Jerram, our jolly, jokey First Assistant Director, we compare health notes. Brian is still chesty but cheerful. I'm still disjointed but dreaming of a chiropractor's magical adjustment. As Claudio in *Measure for Measure* observes, "The miserable have no other medicine / But only hope." Fortunately, Pat discovers a gym, recently opened by a Berkeley graduate in art who, like the Swedish waitress, has also found her paradise here. Daniella, who massaged Pat last year, is now working here and gives me a welcome workover; this time I feel the benefits.

Lunch at Sora Tutta where I celebrated my *Omega* birthday: delicious spit-roasted lamb for me and a salad (and pane cotta) for my gymnast spouse. An American couple there hail and greet me like old friends, setting my memory banks into frantic overdrive. Should I know them? Where did we last meet? Et cetera. It turns out, however, that they are honeymooners and, despite all the ambient high culture, just want to meet Austin Powers' shagadelic boss!

The weather turns heavy and oppressive, and the country peace is shattered by someone firing a gun. Our hotel room presses in on us and we escape for a walk. "Most of the evils of life arise from man's inability to sit still in a room," Blaise Pascal observed and, indeed, I become uncharacteristically jaded, afflicted momentarily with a mild case of locationitis. This can manifest in strange and unexpected ways.

I recently filmed in Las Vegas, and one day, overwhelmed by the ambient nonstop hype and glitz, similarly rushed out of my hotel room. Flagging down a passing taxi, I requested to be transported to the tranquility of the nearby pristine desert. By extraordinary chance, I had lucked on the one cabdriver in this raucous honky-tonk metropolis who regularly went to the adjacent wilderness to meditate. Under his guidance, and the desert's beauty and calm, I felt my pounding pulse return to normal.

Locationitis can metastasize into a major malady. In the Philippines, we once visited a restaurant frequented by the *Apocalypse Now* film crew. The obliging manager had allowed them all to let off pent-up steam by smashing up the place. The damage was paid for — and the process duly repeated!

I tell Pat that I wouldn't be upset if she returned to the States now. Her response is that, as usual, she's going to make the most of it, working on her screenplay and working out, with perhaps that trip to Milan on the weekend. Brightening, I suggest — somewhat unrealistically — that we can drive there together in our Scénic tin can.

That evening, Udo accompanies me back to the castle to film the reverse of the battlement "Bring it on!" scene we shot on that first day in Rome. It's his birthday, and having sincerely inscribed, "To My Megiddan Doppelganger," I give him my Shakespeare book. David Waelder, the sound mixer, replays our first performance, which we now have to match. We discuss the task of also matching in our playing Matt's spiritual vision with Brian's partiality for making a "Gothic horror movie."

There's another popular-song-size silver moon over the lake which, I hope, portends more lyrical weather. Pat and I try to stay up for the third presidential debate, but. . .

WEDNESDAY, OCTOBER 18TH

Waking early, I lie in the filtered sunlight daydreaming travel plans. I'm now convinced that we should fly home to LA directly and not try to include stops in London (to see family) or New York (to see theater). My niece's wedding is coming up in early November, and I resolve to return for that, when all the clans will be gathered. It will be a quick turn-around, but if Udo can do it, so can I! Also, my neck is still giving me concern, and I need to get it fixed by someone reliable before the final week of filming back at the mesa. Having made a decision, I feel better.

A magnificent, golden morning awaits us, and it's all to be enjoyed as I'm not filming till later. We drive to Sutri where the autumn's mellow fruitfulness is evident in the mounds of mushrooms for sale. There's also an impressive amphitheater, complete with still-comfortable seats carved out of the solid rock — one of the few monuments dedicated to live use by the death-enamored Etruscans.

That afternoon, doom is in the air during the shooting of "dear old Dad's" death scene with David Hedison. We finish rehearsing when disaster strikes — the smile is quite literally knocked off my face. Biting open a packet of cookies, I hear an explosive pop as a porcelain cap on one of my front teeth shatters, bequeathing me a jagged — one could say devilish — fang!

Practicing in a mirror, I try to talk without revealing my deformity, but I am unsuccessful — and the upcoming scene, where I taunt and abuse my father, has a great deal of toothsome dialogue. My plight is communicated to the production office, provoking immediate cries of *Emergenza!* and *Dentista!* I decline the option of being treated in Rome — it would have chewed up our charged schedule — and instead rush round, still in evening dress, to the local Bracciano dentist.

The waiting room is full of mums and kids who eye me with polite curiosity. The two dentists on duty immediately abandon what they are doing to attend to me. Once de-fanged, a new fascia is painted on my existing tooth and fixed into permanence with ultraviolet light. The concentration is intense: At intervals each operative steps back to check progress, dabbing here and removing there, like artists creating a masterpiece. Their face masks prevent me from interpreting reactions, and the worst scenarios — mostly variations on "an eye for an eye, and a tooth for a tooth" — flood my imagination.

Finally it's time to rinse and spit — and, taking a deep breath, to view their handiwork. This time the mirror reveals a minor miracle. Although I'm a little long in the tooth, its color is identical to its neighbors. There are genuine "*Grazie milles*" and, on my jubilant way out, I'm introduced to the waiting room as "*Il famoso attore!*" I flash the assembly my new dazzling, confident smile, make a small bow, and return to my place in front of the camera. We film till 11:00 PM when pizza is served — but I'm too scared to eat!

THURSDAY, OCTOBER 19TH

Noah is departing — but not as precipitously as he arrived, as he's decided to linger in Rome. "Gather ye rosebuds while ye may," I murmur, having once been in his identical shoes in the sixties when briefly all roads led to Rome's film capital. The presiding geniuses were such masters as Visconti, Antonioni, and Fellini, whose fantasies were fleshed out by such dazzling stars as Monica Vitti and Marcello Mastroianni.

My own contribution to world cinema this morning constitutes my introduction in *Megiddo*. Typically, I'm making yet another speech, this time at the dedication of the Military Academy's concert hall, in the presence of my father, my brother, my wife, and assembled dignitaries. I'm supposed to look younger so I've allowed my hair to flop youthfully over my face, Hugh Grant–style, hoping that this will also detract attention from my new dentistry, of which I'm acutely self-conscious. David Hedison, in contrast, has "aged up" and now sports the patina of a patriarchal white beard. Our extras look improbably glamorous in their breakfast-time ball gowns, drinking hot coffee to keep warm in the still-chilly castle confines.

I lunch with Michael Biehn in the mobile restaurant, located in the depths of the ancient moat and staffed by a bevy of lively girls. He recounts his adventures on the road. Taking our advice, he enjoyed an epicurean meal at the Cipriani Hotel in Venice. After this brush with high society, however he came rudely down to earth by taking a bus from Siena back to Rome.

That evening Dad's death scene, in which he is hurled

by me from an upper story into the stony courtyard, is mercifully problem free. I'm always uneasy when a stunt has to be performed, having witnessed too many accidents — and experienced many myself. There was that high dive from a crashing zeppelin into four feet of concrete-bottomed water in Malta, and countless swashbuckling instances in the *Musketeer* movie when my stunt double was injured, obliging me to double for him! David Hedison and I have even ended up with bruises and bumps just manhandling each other to the parapet.

The stunt fall onto a pile of collapsible cardboard boxes goes perfectly, to mass exhalations of relief. Afterward we film the scene where we surround the dying patriarch, rehearsed so self-consciously on Matt's dining room floor all those weeks ago. It now has its own logic, born of our characters' organic growth. Part of this evolution comes almost too late when, kneeling over my father's body, I discover on the very last take a sound that is a perfect cross between a sob and a snicker. I *like* being Stone!

FRIDAY, OCTOBER 20TH

The late night engenders a free morning. (Most contracts stipulate a ten- or twelve-hour turnaround.) We drive to Anguilera for a stroll along its scenic lakeside promenade. Dogs and cats doze in the sun; an old woman sells walnuts fresh from her tree. We lunch in a restaurant run by two expatriate ladies, one from as far afield as New Zealand. They have obviously found their bliss here too in "thou paradise of exiles, Italy," to echo the poet Shelley who, reputedly, once had the same rooms as myself at Oxford. The food is ambrosial, the equal of anything for which Michael Biehn might have bankrupted himself in Venice, and fully justifying that overused and now worthless term, "gourmet."

The postprandial filming is, fortunately, not particularly taxing — close-up shots of blood dripping from fingers — and I expend most energy in thinking up appropriate responses for our next setup, when Michael and his Ranger troops invade my castle. Most are variations on the usual sarcastic, fraternal put-down, such as: "Ah, brother dear, I've been expecting you. Please get those filthy boots off my Aubusson carpet." We end up filming them all.

Brian and I also discuss Gabriella's "torture" scene. I'm still strongly convinced it should be a mental, rather than physical, assault — provoking something akin to Lady M's descent into sleepwalking madness.

SATURDAY, OCTOBER 21ST

It's the weekend and, unusual for most foreign location films, we have the luxury of two free days. I drive with Pat through the gilded haze northward to Orvieto. En route we pass a car crash, jogging painful memories of our own vehicular mishaps in Italy. There was that head-on crash with a truck in deepest Calabria that sent Pat to the hospital in Rome and which is still imprinted on my scarred smile. Pat's recuperation from broken ribs was not helped by my giving her Marty Feldman's hilarious script of *The Last Remake of Beau Geste* to read, which, unfortunately, proved to be, literally, sidesplittingly funny. Instinctively, I slow down to enjoy the life-affirming views, recalling, too, a road sign once spotted in Jamaica: "Undertakers like Overtakers"!

We pass Viterbo and the turnoff to Bomarzo where, on

the last shoot, we visited the fabulous Monster Park created by Duke Orsini in the sixteenth century. Here, stone fantasies of giants and devils inhabit a nightmare landscape. It now sets me wondering if evil, the kind that drives Gabriella mad, can ever be convincingly depicted.

I know that it can be felt — and never more potently and convincingly than when Pat and I visited Bucharest and its chilling Palace of the People, formerly occupied by the deposed dictator Ceaucescu. By chance Pat was carrying a pendulum, which the latent malevolence caused to spin negatively almost out of her hand like a demented whirling dervish.

Conversely, I know that goodness can also be divined. Once, after a traumatic experience in Spain, Pat's anguish was eased when she glimpsed an angel protecting her. I have filmed in Medjugorje, Croatia, where the Virgin Mary appeared to local children, infusing the place with an undeniably spiritual atmosphere despite the ensuing hordes of pilgrims.

And I know that evil has a smell. In August 1999, the gigantic *Amorphophallus Titanum* plant, the world's largest flower, had its first ever blooming in California at the local Huntington Library and Botanical Garden. Among thousands of others, I made the pilgrimage there to inhale the "corpse flower's" incomparably disgusting odor of rotting flesh — the perfect nosegay for our Beast.

From afar, Orvieto greets us like an illustration in a fairy story. Here I once-upon-a-time had a driver who got so drunk that I commandeered his car, putting him on a bus as he refused to drive back to Rome with us. The "theft" of his vehicle having been reported to the police, I was arrested on the *autostrada* and brought back to the Orvieto police station. There, my would-be chauffeur ruined his case — and most of his clothing — by suddenly jumping through a plate glass window.

It's so hot having lunch on a terrace opposite the magnificent decorated facade of the cathedral that we soon seek refuge within the forests of marble columns in its cool interior. The Signorelli chapel overwhelms as we sit and contemplate his powerful depiction of the Last Judgement, with devils at least as fearsome as our own computer-generated horrors. Given Stone's relentless loquacity, Old Nick must be a formidable windbag — Signorelli has even painted an image of the Antichrist preaching!

We continue northward into deepest Tuscany to Pienza, the medieval papal town where Zeffirelli's *Romeo and Juliet* was also filmed in the romantic summer of 1967. I had just met Pat, and as with the two fictional lovers, our lives instantly and fatefully intertwined. I was cast as Tybalt and she was sent by Vogue to photograph this exquisite recreation of "fair Verona, where we lay our scene." Pat stands again by the fountain upon which Zeffirelli lifted her to obtain a vantage point for capturing some of the nine pages of color photos that Vogue unprecedentedly printed.

Revisiting the Palazzo Piccolomini, with its charming courtyard and loggia that stood in for the Capulet house, Pat photographs me again in the same place where Tybalt's dead body was deposed. Cries of both lamentation and laughter haunt the air, mingling with memories of stately dance music and candlelit feasting. Outside, the sound of swords and the swirl of dust still hang in the narrow streets lined with shops that now cater to contending mobs of thronging tourists.

We press on to Bagno Vignone, where we had stayed during the filming. My hotel, the Posta Marcucci, has now grown from a modest family inn into a large spa. The man at reception recognizes me: "I used to watch you practice your duels in our garden." His aunts still rule the roost, one of them sitting by the door, like Juliet's nurse, reading through a large magnifying glass. While some Americans bawl bonhomie at each other, he confides that he's fed up with having to speak English now that the place has been discovered!

The hotel is certainly fully booked, but he insists that we take a bath in its outside thermal pool. I remember doing this after a long day's duelling and feeling the bruises and tension simply evaporate away. A brochure apostrophizes the virtues of "this peace full enchanted place of health" that "cheers the atmosphere with its warm sulphur springs which rise from the earth, known for 2000 year." Lorenzo de Medici used to come here to appease "the family sorrow in tepid water," and nowadays Roberto Benigni writes all his screenplays here. We follow in their famous footsteps, wallowing in the warmth while enjoying the panoramic view over the Val d'Orcia.

Other great spa experiences ease into one's mellowing consciousness: the ornate art *nouveau* temple of a bath at the Gellert Hotel in Budapest, hammams in North Africa, and invigorating seaweed and saltwater therapies in France. Feeling fantastic after only a short dip, we make vows to return yet again for longer stays. After dining in the same little hotel where Pat had stayed and where I used to echo Romeo's passionate "It is my lady; O, it is my love!," we find a delightfully simple room in a nearby inn.

SUNDAY, OCTOBER 22ND

At a local jewelers, I buy Pat a necklace — the significance of it coming from here enhances its beauty. We drive on past bare, plowed fields to Montalcino, famous for its red wine, and on to Siena for lunch in the Campo, the fan-shaped main square. This is where the famous horse race, the Palio, is held; years ago I had the good fortune to witness it, an unforgettable explosion of flags and horseflesh, color and excitement. Now the hot sun has drawn people to the open space as if to the beach; they lie stripped and stretched on the warm stones, while waves of tourists wash through them. The cacophony from the guides' contending loudspeakers, however, disturbs the peace, creating a permanent Palio uproar.

Seeking refuge off the beaten tourist track, we find it in the exquisite Oratorio of San Bernardino. We have the place to ourselves: It's so quiet that you can almost hear the painted angels sing. "The traveller sees what he sees, the tourist sees what he has come to see," G.K. Chesterton observed. Cocooned in privilege, I would like to think that we number among the former; but the pile of guides, brochures, postcards, car keys, cameras, and packages of the local *panforte* delicacy we are carrying witness our irrefutable affiliation to the latter!

MONDAY, 23RD OCTOBER

Back in Bracciano, the weekend's glorious golden weather persists — also its theme of religious art. In a beautiful castle room that features a large painting of the crucifixion, we film the moment where the Antichrist mocks Jesus. The special lens has arrived that will enable us to photograph in a split ratio, with both Christ and myself in focus. I stick with my earlier decision to play the scene very quietly in contrast to all the preceding speechifying. Also — if the edited order remains the same — the exultant "Bowl of Wrath" duet with Udo on the battlements that follows it.

Burt Dunk has a problem, fortunately not so much with his eyes but his ears, which a doctor treats on set. Again, an involuntary pause is put to creative ends. Some extra dialogue is required to motivate my rising and crossing to address directly the portrait of Christ. "The Devil can quote scripture to his own ends," Shakespeare observed, and we ransack Matt's Bible for something suitable. Exactly what is needed is found in the Book of Daniel: "Woe to the inhabitants of the earth and the sea! For the Devil has come down to you, having great wrath — because he knows that he has a short time."

All this prompts more memories of playing John the Baptist, chained up in that freezing Tunisian dungeon.

When Zeffirelli asked me to "improvise" some dialogue, divine inspiration sent me to the Book of Isaiah for his incomparable oratory.

It is Pat's last night in Italy and she invites the Crouch family to share it at a farewell dinner. Most restaurants are closed today, but our favorite little family place by the lake in Trevignano is as welcoming as ever. Conversation naturally turns to our film and all that has happened so far — the problems and the passions, the egos and the ecstasy.

Matt tells me that with this film, he is taking more interest in the artistic side, the acting and directing. However, he's a born marketer, and having supervised *The Omega Code*'s production and release, he's now raring to do the same with its sequel in the long and complex post-production process. His ambition and enthusiasm are infectious — he's like a benign Stone Alexander, out to conquer the world!

We raise our glasses anew to our growing friendship and a glowing future.

CHAPTER NINE

Ceasefire

TUESDAY, OCTOBER 24TH

I drive with Pat through misty fields and quiet villages down
to the busy modern airport and — "parting is such sweet
sorrow" — a fond farewell embrace. It's wonderful to be
married to someone who is a partner as well as a companion, there to share both the rough and the smooth. I have
witnessed at firsthand the emotional trauma and compromise attendant on the long periods of separation that so
many actors have to endure, and I have counted my bless-
ings. I wish my wife a safe trip — and an uneventful one,
for we share souvenirs of other more hair-raising journeys.

There were the two bizarre glass-eating flights across the Pacific. One was to Japan just after Pat had swallowed some ice cream filled with broken glass. Informed we had to wait a critical time to ascertain that her internal organs — the same ones that, ironically, Pat now so lovingly photographs — were still intact, this breath-baited waiting provided our endless in-flight entertainment. Then, on a more recent trip to Hong Kong to participate in the Colony's hand-over ceremonies, history repeated itself in midair with her broken dessert dish. The pilot even radioed a doctor back in Chicago for advice, no doubt to calm his own shattered nerves.

Then there was the time when Pat cut her head while photographing in the unfinished Getty Museum, the next day flying to London with her wound covered in Chinese herbs and swathed in a turban, and going from Heathrow to Harley Street to get it treated. But not even these incidents were as strange as the one featuring the sweet little white-haired old lady who, sitting smiling benignly behind us on a flight to Australia, suddenly turned into a mini-Stone, projectile vomiting like a possessed fiend so relentlessly and violently that the whole cabin had to be fumigated and later refurbished. But I certainly never worry about Pat travelling alone. Unfailingly, someone will always carry her bags and even volunteer to drive her to her destination.

I'm missing her already, her pioneering enthusiasm and passion for life, and my Paganini piece takes on a melancholy overtone. Luigi, however, is encouraging. It turns out that, somewhat improbably, he's also a judo champion, so I'm glad I haven't provoked him too much! I persuade Luigi to record the piece himself so that the playback is not just an academic rendition, but an individually expressive and sensual serenade. Afterward, I feel strangely tired — is this just end-of-film ennui, or the continuing results of an off-keel cranium?

WEDNESDAY, OCTOBER 2ND

As I get up, Pat calls from LA to say that she's just going to bed — and that her flight was fine. The light on the lake seems less golden and more leaden. Flies are suddenly everywhere — perhaps I've inherited the ones that buzzed John Fasano farewell. I breakfast with young Cody Crouch who, despite his tender years, is an habitual early-riser. Our conversation turns to coin collecting and he's delighted — "cool" is his precise verbal reaction — when I hand over my assortment of Belgian change.

Michael Biehn and Gil Colon who, like Udo and myself, play so many scenes together, check out of the hotel in tandem. Like a real soldier, Gil must be glad to be going home after this posting abroad: He's missing his wife and young sons.

Last night Brian and I discussed whether, in the final encounter, I should kill Gil, as in the script. His is one of the few African-American characters in our film, and Brian was concerned that my shooting him should not be tainted with misinterpolated racist overtones. My feeling is that the killing is unnecessary, given the power of the dramatic clash between Stone and David already filmed. We have also established that Stone is too grand to do his own slaughter. Gil should do something heroic on the mesa, I suggest, when we return there next week for more battle scenes.

That evening the "dawn" violin scene is filmed up on the castle battlements with their stupendous views. I serenade

Diane at the perfect time — just as the sun is setting in a vibrant sky. It goes so fast that there's no time to rehearse and we grab the shot, *allegro con fuoco,* in two takes. Luigi, who provided the playback track, beams approvingly. Diane has now finished her role and, congratulating her, I give her this time a genuine, not a stage, farewell kiss.

There's more filming that night, but many of us repair to a local restaurant for an impromptu, celebratory last supper. Breaking with discipline, and in echo of our battlement scene, I pour out the bowls of vintage — I don't care how bad it makes me feel tomorrow. Dario, our Tuscan assistant director, is a great wine connoisseur and he selects one that thrills my uneducated and neglected palate. Matt and I talk about a publicity film to be shot with me back on the mesa, and Stephan and I arrange to finalize its script over the weekend back in LA. I suddenly feel redundant again and slip away, abandoning everyone to the night's big military manoeuvres.

Back in the Alfredo I pack away the life of the last few, charged weeks. Having spent so much of my career in an array of accommodations — from a Japanese country inn, sleeping on the floor with fish soup for breakfast, to a castle in Ireland, spit-roasting salmon for supper; from the Ritz in Paris to a tent pitched high in the Himalayas, and from behind velvet swags to behind the Iron Curtain itself — I'm grateful for the pleasures provided by my present modest rooms.

Location shooting can expose nerves as well as film. I remember the earthquake that shook us out of bed in the Philippines, and the yacht that we crewed as our floating home while filming in the Caribbean, that hit a reef off St. Lucia. As a young actor, I filmed many times in the former Yugoslavia. There was a mythic story then circulating London that if you were offered a film in this country, you could phone a certain hot line and be counselled out of accepting!

But nothing has ever been quite as bad as the circumstances surrounding a film that a friend once made in some obscure provincial backwater of the former Soviet Union. Conditions were so grim that sanity was only saved by an enterprising old actor who had been imprisoned by the Germans in the last war. Taking charge, he disciplined and organized his men as if they were back in the Stalag! The mental pressures of being cooped up together day and night can prove overwhelming. As Mark Twain sagely ob-served, "I have found out there ain't no way to find out whether you like people or hate them than to travel with them."

THURSDAY, OCTOBER 26TH

Pat calls just after I make the morning's first delicious cup of strong tea. She's had a full day: hair cut, book party, dinner with friends, and a head start on demolishing our very own high mesa of amassed mail.

Breakfasting by the window, I watch incoming rain clouds overshadow the sky. Jerram joins me with an eye-popping report of what happened on the very last take of the night-shoot. Apparently, a special effects explosion went off too soon, setting one of our US Rangers alight. It looked spectacular — the kind of shot one usually spent hours preparing. The enflamed extra, thank goodness, was not hurt. The stunt co-ordinator, however, was not so fortunate — he fainted dead away! All this boosts Brian's reputation as a "hot" director — one earned in his early pyromaniac days when he invented a fire retardant that he put to the test on television, literally lighting up the screen by setting himself ablaze!

I settle "*il conto,*" say my heartfelt "*arrivedercis*" and "*grazies*" and head off to Fiumicino airport where the traveller is welcomed by the huge statue of my former mentor, Leonardo da Vinci. There's rumor of an air traffic controllers' strike tomorrow, so I'm even more grateful to be slipping away now.

Germany greets us with the glowing autumnal forests around Frankfurt. While waiting for the LA flight, I amuse myself by watching respectable businessmen filch chocolate bars in the lounge like naughty schoolboys. Telephoning my parents, I learn that I've just been made a great uncle to little Joe, the first offspring of my doctor niece, Kate and her equally brilliant medic husband, Mike. This presents an even greater incentive to return for the wedding especially as this latest relative will be there, too.

On the plane, an elderly former Director of the Los Angeles Philharmonic is sitting opposite me. He flew here just four days ago, he tells me, and after a brief interval back in LA, will head down to Australia. This makes me now resolved to bounce back for the nuptials.

We take off into the sunset — will it last all the way to that far West Coast? There's caviar on the menu — a little dab of it — and I enjoy it while I can. How much longer can we indulgent few feast on endangered species? There's even a porno film on the video menu — you have to credit the Germans for being broad-minded!

I muse on the time when, travelling to India, *The Three Musketeers* was the in-flight movie. The chief steward deemed it only appropriate that I move up to first class to view my film — an invitation that was gallantly accepted! I think of that recent *New Yorker* cartoon where a pilot announces: "The flight today is five hours in first class and twelve and a half in coach."

Much as I hate to see movies butchered into discolored small-screen format like kids' video games, I watch one, but it's not good. I try to be generous, knowing all the ambition, devotion, stress, and heartache that inevitably went into making it. When and where did it start to go wrong?

Although those other "brief chroniclers of the time," the critics, may disbelieve this, no one ever sets out to make a bad movie. People often ask me if I can tell how a movie will turn out while making it, and I honestly reply that I can't. Good films tend to happen despite, rather than because of, circumstances. It's all in the lap of the gods — or, to use a more basic term, a film shoot is one big, glorious crapshoot.

But all these neurotic reflections are now too close to home. I lie back and let relaxing symphonic music sweep through my padded, noise-eliminating ear phones — equipment as indispensable as the little germ-busting ionizing machine worn when flying. Fortunately my seat companion totally ignores me. There's no showbiz inquisition, and especially, no vehement insistence, against all my polite denials, that I was in a certain film, to the point that I begin to doubt myself! There's no shaking of hands — so often in the middle of meals — and no tapping of computer keys, the contemporary equivalent of the Chinese water torture.

I update this journal, paying homage to Oscar Wilde's declaration, "I never travel without my diary. One should always have something sensational to read on the train!" I enjoy airborne writing when one's imagination seems to take off and become pressurized too. My best work ever was, of course, done on the Concorde!

It's warm and comfortable: For me, true torture is a long flight in an over air-conditioned plane, the perfect illustration of the concept of hell freezing over. I stretch out under a blanket and am soon asleep. . . and awake to see LA equally stretched out like an urban blanket with its regular pattern of freeways and factories, palm trees and swimming pools. The architecture looks mostly flimsy and gimcrack. "Travelling is the ruin of all happiness," Fanny Burney, the eightenth-century English novelist, observed, "There's no looking at a building here after seeing Italy."

FRIDAY, OCTOBER 27TH

Between unpacking and answering phone calls and letters, I arrange my return to Europe in a week's time — how strange to be doing this within hours of arriving home. What perverse wandering planet rules my birth sign?

This is the first day without a direct connection with the film — apart from the constant mental one. I think of our valiant company, hoping they are not strike-bound. I repair to Marc, my chiropractor who, as he puts it, "pulls my neck out of my head." That alone, he confirms, would account for my persistent tiredness.

SATURDAY, OCTOBER 28TH

Brian calls and we review next week's work, especially the crucial pre-battle encounter between Stone and David. I argue that Stone can't be surprised by his brother when tracked down at the end — the Antichrist is, after all, omniscient. I suggest using a double, as Hitler, Eisenhower, and Montgomery did.

Tonight we are invited to one of the major Hollywood charity events of the year, the Carousel of Hope Ball. Pat has donated a photo to the silent auction — it's a favorite of mine: David Hockney painting his seminal "Mulholland Drive."

The event at the Beverly Hilton Hotel has drawn the town, and we take in the usual celebrity suspects. A great deal of expensive dentistry — but no better than my Bracciano brand — is flashed at us. (Ever neurotic, I have already checked and my tooth is indeed a millimeter too long!) Ahead of us, running the gauntlet of photographers is Julia Louis-Dreyfus, who informs me of her young son's career choice — after watching *The Three Musketeers* he's decided to enlist in their ranks! I compliment her on her wonderful performance in *Seinfeld,* and I wonder what it must be like to play the same role for a decade.

I run into leading ladies of my own — Jackie Bisset and Jane Seymour. Jane is with her husband, James Keach, who was my understudy in *Outcry* on Broadway. As we progress into dinner, James and I chorus the opening monologue to some baffled stares. There's Jackie Collins and Dustin Hoffman, and we pass Jon Voight with Liam Neeson. An actress whom I *should* recognize, coincidentally waxes lyrical about my *Romeo and Juliet,* and I recount our recent adventures in Zeffirelli-land. There's Sydney Poitier lending dignity to the proceedings, and James Coburn tells us he's off to France for a film festival. What a carousel of a profession!

At dinner, Jay Leno is the host and his jokes come hard,

fast, and waspish, as if Stone himself had somehow meta-morphosed into a stand-up comedian. Not even President Clinton, emulating the media-astute Alexander and present electronically, can top him — despite slipping in such weird double entendres as claiming to be "still on the job." His words not exactly received in reverent silence, he's followed by the official entertainers. These include the talented Charlotte Church — now sounding and looking more Charlie's Angel than angelic — and the equally youthful Latin heartthrob, Ricky Martin. His music is so head-throbbingly loud, however, that we find it hard to enjoy. Perhaps all that lakeside calm has over-sensitized our hearing.

SUNDAY, OCTOBER 29TH

Awake at 5:30 thinking about that final encounter with David. I'm convinced now that it is best done deviously with a double.

Pat and I go for a favorite walk in Franklin Canyon, a pristine wilderness a mere stone's throw from the jungle of boutiques and thickets of traffic in fashionable Beverly Hills. It seems unnaturally quiet and deserted until I realize that we have gained an hour with the seasonal time change.

I call Brian, who agrees to give the Devil his due. Parallel with David's arrival and arrest, he will film Stone in his command tent surrounded by a bevy of military brass, politicians, and camp-following courtesans (or "whores of Babylon," as Brian describes them). The skies thunder agreement — it starts to pour with rain as we drive out to an uncharacteristically windswept and sodden Malibu for a friend's beachside wedding. Why does this film affect weather so weirdly?

That evening another good friend, Professor Philip Bobbitt, arrives from Austin, Texas, to stay. An erstwhile government advisor, he's just completed a mammoth book on military strategy, so our conversations are as timely as they are intriguing. "The best thing about Armageddon," he offers, "is that there will be no subsequent Peace Conference. These are notorious for provoking the resumption of hostilities!"

MONDAY, OCTOBER 30TH

Much of the day is spent in tidying up the house for tonight's dinner party for John Major. Domestic chores, after such an interval, prove almost enjoyable; it's certainly a pleasure to see our home respond to this unwonted attention and turn into a lady of the night herself, both glamorous and seductively welcoming.

Our very own World Leader scene that evening is immensely enjoyable — and speech-free, for once, from me! I hang on John's words: It's a privilege to have insight into the mind of a man who, politically, actually did what I'm now only playing at doing. The conversation goes on till 1:00 AM, but reluctantly, I retire early as there's reveille on the mesa at 0600 hours.

TUESDAY, OCTOBER 31ST

I'm awakened what seems five minutes later at 4:45 AM — except that it's 3:45, as I've forgotten to adjust my alarm to the hour change. Given this timely bonus, I use it to enjoy a leisurely drive under the bright stars. The rain has scrubbed the sky clean and the extravagant dawn is unfiltered and in sharp focus. But it's cold — 37°. The new scene in the tent plays well. Feeling that slightly detached relaxation experienced when tired, I pick out and flirt with one of the "ladies." With Gabriella's death so present in the audience's mind this should make Stone's behavior doubly offensive.

Pat and Philip arrive for lunch, and like a tour guide, I show off the encircling panoramas. Visitors to film sets usually expect something immediately entertaining to take place, and they are invariably disappointed. It's the end, not the means to it, that satisfies. Equally, interviewers always ask for details of "something amusing that happened on the set." I'm usually at a loss to oblige, although today I can provide good value with explosions and stunt men flying off their air-ramp launches like circus artists. There's shooting in every sense of the word — militaristic as well as cinematic — with war games for Philip to watch and analyze.

All this is in realization of the prophecy in Revelation (16:16): "And he gathered them together into a place called in the Hebrew tongue Armageddon." The desert is filled with troops and ordnance, like outtakes from a Gulf War documentary. Some three thousand conscripts, like Matt's legions of "Prayer Warriors," have volunteered for this last battle.

While the main company was away in Europe, Paul Lombardi and his team of pyrotechnicians rigged the mesa for battle. Roads were widened and miles of cable laid, connecting a whole arsenal of explosive devices. Fifty battlefield vehicles, including tanks, half-tracks, armored personnel carriers, and jeeps, were transported to the site. The contending armies can even be differentiated by their weaponry — the Americans use Bradley tanks while Stone deploys their British counterpart, Centurions.

Earlier, I had filmed the behind-the-scenes documentary, improvising on a text prepared by Stephan. I was also interviewed by our Supreme Commander, Paul Crouch, who, costumed in full military uniform, looked even more magnificent than Stone Alexander. Uncertain whether to shake hands or salute him, I complimented him on his son's own splendid generalship.

The huge scene brings into sharp focus the sheer ambition of our epic movie — the attempt to represent the greatest, and arguably the most important, battle ever to be fought. Making the biblical word flesh has proved both popular and daunting for generations of filmmakers. "I had a terrible time," John Huston is reported as saying about his *The Bible,* especially filming the Creation and Noah's Flood scenes, "I really don't know how God managed it!"

Feeling that old, familiar emotion of relief mixed with regret at having finished the filming part of my role, I drive home as the freeway's arteries begin their evening's sclerotic clogging. An invitation to accompany Philip and Pat to a Halloween party is declined. After wearing a costume for such a long day, I'm reluctant to put on another. I'm in the mood for an instant treat — a long, lazy hot bath — not the trick of further enforced socializing. I present Philip with my black high-buttoned velvet jacket from *The Omega Code* — how appropriate to go dressed as the Devil! And how more appropriate than to finish on this day when, in pre-Christian times, the night was ruled by witches and warlocks, those close kissing cousins to Stone Alexander.

I reflect on everything it has taken to wage our war to this point, and on how much I look forward to the equally strategic post-production engagements ahead. So far, the movie has provided another life-enhancing experience and I thank "the Divinity that shapes our ends" for doing so in such an instructive, entertaining, and beguiling way.

CHAPTER TEN

Armistice

After this whirlwind week at home, I fly back to Europe on a plane that, with elegant consistency, breaks down in Chicago. A film producer friend is also aboard, going to London — for the day — to meet with an actor. What performer, I wonder, could possibly warrant such expenditure of energy.

We wait — and wait — in a benighted airport for a replacement plane; then one passenger also breaks down and, like Peter Finch in *Network,* screams that he's mad as hell and is not going to take it any more. The police are called and our gallant, eloquent spokesman is taken away while we eventually take off.

Landfall is over the rocky splinters of western Ireland so familiar from childhood holidays and grown-up movie-making. Here Pat and I once lived in a castle — a tiny turret compared to Stone's towering pile — during the filming of *Alfred the Great,* when I also commanded an army, but this time from horseback. Belatedly, our plane sweeps in over a city of London already glowing in another sunset.

Renting an unfamiliar car I drive to Canterbury in the now pitch dark more by luck and instinct, alongside mammoth trucks spewing from the Channel Tunnel and charging into commerce like our massed tanks at Megiddo. "Forth, pilgrim, forth! Forth, Beste, out of they stal! / Know thy contree, look up, thank God of al!" as Geoffrey Chaucer exhorted. Eventually arriving at the ancient walled city, I put up, quite appropriately, at the charmingly old-fashioned Chaucer hotel. There's even something I haven't seen since childhood, a stone hot water bottle in the bed!

The wedding of my niece Lucy to her James is a full fantasy one, with hats and tailcoats and the bridal pair arriving at the church in an old crock taxi in rare, bright sunshine. Lucy, an overworked and underpaid nurse in the National Health System, thoroughly deserves such spoiling, though I keep expecting a worried Hugh Grant to appear and make an embarrassed speech!

Showbiz is certainly in evidence when, at one point in the service, the priest asks us all to applaud. Outside, it remains dry and windless, which is just as well as the reception is in a large tent pitched on someone's damp lawn. I feel like a tourist in my native land. "The whole object of travel is not to set foot on foreign land;" I'm reminded by G.K. Chesterton, "it is at last to set foot in one's own country as a foreign land."

Enjoying the Englishness of it all, I marvel at the quantities of beer being downed and the sheer size of today's youth. There are funny speeches, diligently worked on and delivered, as well as happy tribal reunions. I particularly relish photographing my father holding his new great-grandson, little Joe, a moving testament to Tagore's observation that, "Each new child is a reminder that God has not lost hope in man." A big bonfire is lit, anticipating the morrow's Guy

Fawkes Day, and inflaming boyhood memories of satanic conflagrations with rocket-flared skies, whirling Catherine wheels, big bangs, and baked potatoes in the embers.

The next day, *Alfred the Great* turns up yet again in the most unexpected place. Deciding to revisit Canterbury Cathedral, I'm astonished to find it closed on a Sunday — for a service! A church warden, curly-haired and cassocked "that hadde a fyr-reed cherubinnes face" yields to my entreaties to be allowed inside "for a quick prayer" and opens a side chapel entirely for myself.

As an ex-choir boy who grew to love the sheer theatricality of the high Anglican service, I enjoy hearing again the great words that, alongside Shakespeare, shaped our language. Mingling with the music, they echo around the ancient building that, like its Flemish and Italian cousins, is a masterpiece of faith and spirit fused in stone and glass. The price of admission is an autograph for my benefactor's girlfriend, "an Austin Powers fan."

The official opening time of the cathedral is now imminent, and I employ the interim in viewing its new audio-visual presentation. The opening sequence shows the

building being sacked and pillaged by Danish invaders —
led, I am astonished to see, by myself as King Guthrum
yelling the very same Viking war cry that protected us in
Rio. "Is *nothing* sacred?"

I drive to my sister Penny's lovely Georgian house in
Faversham, by the wide Thames estuary, where she enter-
tains some of the wedding guests to yet another meal. It's
like a replay of that first Bracciano Sunday lunch with its
lively mixture of generations, including the very next one
for, around me, young nieces and cousins nurse babies like
so many Madonnas. My father crowns the occasion by making an eloquent and emotional speech that I wouldn't have
missed for the world.

I leave reluctantly for London, reached after a long crawl
in torrential rain through its southern suburbs where I grew
up and where the ambition to be an actor first flared. Old
memories are revived, to combine with vivid new ones like
movie flashbacks in a headlong narrative.

Next day I visit the Royal Academy of Arts to see its
challenging *Apocalypse* show. Those controversial brothers,
Jake and Dinos Chapman, have an exhibit called *Hell* that

is chillingly haunting and genuinely frightening — display cases, like glass coffins, arranged in a swastika formation and full of miniature figures torturing, slaughtering, and dismembering in a dreadful prison camp setting. They have the same nightmarish quality as the effects we have been trying to achieve cinematically. I think of my father's distressing — and reluctantly revealed — reports of seeing Auschwitz and Belsen as a soldier, on his way to Berlin and his own last battle with the Nazis. I'm so repelled, yet impressed by this artwork that I consider calling Matt to suggest that a camera panning over it could create an appropriately horrific title sequence for our film.

Afterwards, still sporting my producer's hat, I meet with some distributors about the long-overdue British release of *The Omega Code.* That evening, solemnly intoned reports of an accident to the Queen Mother lead the news, pushing next day's US election into obscurity. There'll always be an England!

The land I return to on election day, however, is at least as eccentric as the one I have just left — especially the slapdash way it goes about choosing its leader. Another form —

the immigration one — highlights the inexplicable American practice of putting the month before the day. There was also the snobbish French pronunciation of "herb" and such baffling linguistic conundrums as driving a car on a parkway and then parking it on a driveway!

I find Washington engulfed in a warm mist and another presidential scandal. Pat and I are reunited at the British Embassy where we are fortunate to be guests. The only Lutyens building in America, it's one of my favorite places, with gracious, unpretentious hosts, Sir Christopher and Lady Meyer, welcoming staff, and the best cup of tea this side of the Continental Divide. I'm in need of one: The airline has lost my bags. Next day, they are served up with breakfast and the newspapers.

The Florida recount has hijacked the headlines, reminding one that there is nothing so fantastic and dramatic as real life. "History on hold," one paper pronounces. It dominates the conversation the following night when history is celebrated. Tina Brown hosts an Embassy dinner for Simon Schama to launch the publication of his *A History of Britain.* I'm a huge admirer of Schama's brilliant mind and on-screen aplomb — and his historical recall. "We met in Amsterdam — in the lobby of an hotel," he reminds me precisely, and we chat warmly about our common circumstance of being expatriate in this former jewel in the British colonial crown.

All the speeches that evening are tinged with the presentiment that we are living through an historic moment. I long to discuss this with Bob Woodward who, sitting across from me, is tantalizingly out of conversational range. The divisiveness is everywhere apparent. Our cheerful eighty-year-old cabdriver, rigid with arthritis, who takes us to the airport, suggests that the candidates should toss a coin for it. How can I explain that the time has come for Stone Alexander's *North American Zone* to make recounts irrelevant and unite the nation?

Back home in LA on the eleventh of November, Armistice Day: an appropriate time to get back in touch with Brian, who has just put an end to the Battle of Armageddon. The very last scene in the movie was completed, like *The Omega Code,* with the sunrise. Apparently, it was so cold on the mesa that ice had to be scraped from the camera dolly tracks. Brian confides that, as Supreme Commander of three thousand volunteer troops, he was terrified that something catastrophic would happen in the dark. Tomorrow he plans to put together some footage for the preliminary marketing campaign.

The following day I take my travel-ravaged clothes in to be cleaned and repaired. Greg, my tailor, tells me a sweet story about his late client and our mutual friend, Cary Grant. Apparently when the business was in its infancy, Cary used to sit in the doorway and, by his stellar presence, would seduce customers into coming in. I recall that he was fond of vacationing in England, staying at modest bed-and-breakfast places. The astonishment of landladies opening their doors to him must have matched that of people espying their screen idol in a humble shop.

A few days later, there's another rite of passage — a "wrap" party to celebrate the completion of filming. It's probably the first time that every production department has been brought together in one place, in this case a local nightclub. Everyone looks strangely glamorous after the stress of filming and being seen for so long in practical work clothes. Cast parties can be slightly unnerving, due to the unaccustomed access to liquor, when inhibitions are sometimes abandoned and opinions unguarded.

The four-minute promotional reel is shown, to much enthusiasm. The film looks huge and ambitious, even without its special effects. Rob's team invites me to watch the upcoming filmed demolition of a sixty-foot-high model of the Colosseum and an equally realistic rendition of the Sphinx. Matt tells me that two million video units of *Left Behind*, a similarly faith-based thriller, have been ordered, confirming that *The Omega Code* was not a flash in the pan but the forerunner of a market trend.

In November, I learn that my father has suffered another stroke. He makes an extraordinary recovery, but I'm forever grateful that I made that decision to return to England. I'm dissuaded from flying back there immediately by my medically oriented relatives who take my father into their competent care. Under it, he continues to improve.

Other memories are revived watching *The Making of Megiddo* on TBN. The crosscutting of the reportage with the movie footage works well. Predictably, John Fasano is good on camera, although I wish he'd had the nerve to perform at least one of his imitations!

At the end of the month, continuing the military theme, we attend a Service's salute to Jack Valenti, our affable Washington Film Supremo. Among the entertainers is a chorus of singing and marching paratroopers. What's next — *Megiddo* the musical? *Never* discount anything. The dress uniforms around us gleaming with gold-braided honors and shiny brass buttons, make our film costumes seem positively drab in contrast.

My Stone tuxedo, though, is put to use again in Washington in early December, celebrating the nation's performing arts at the Kennedy Center Honors. Naturally, in the televised show, the camera chooses to focus in on my face at the precise moment that I lose my way in singing the complex — and for me, unfamiliar — words of *The Star-Spangled Banner.* The rockets' red glare is nothing compared to the embarrassment suffusing my countenance.

The high point of the weekend is a reception at the White House that, in light of the ongoing political uncertainties, has an added piquancy. The event manages to achieve that American paradox of being formal yet friendly, grand and intimate. Farewell thanks, both sincere and otherwise, are made to the retiring leader of the North American Zone — sorry, the United States — as thoughts turn to its unpredictable destiny. It seems that even Clinton's Deputy Secretary of State, Strobe Talbott, had glimpsed the shadow of Stone Alexander over the future. "Within the next hundred years nationhood as we know it will be obsolete;" he predicted, "all states will recognize a single global authority."

We head for New York where I'm interviewed by a writer for an article in *G.Q.* magazine on religion-based films. He has already seen some of *Megiddo*'s footage and professes enthusiasm, but having been bruised by journalists before, my guard is up. I suggest doing the proposed photo shoot at the special effects studio, surrounded by its model monuments and other satanic props.

That evening, I'm invited to talk to the graduate film class at NYU, no doubt addressing some of my future employers. I concentrate on emphasizing the actor's contribution to that vital working relationship, where human needs have to be balanced with technical demands. I tell them I have this fantasy — now swiftly becoming reality — that if computer trends continue evolving, an actor need only report briefly to the studio to get his image recorded, his performance then being digitally created. I'm relieved to learn, though, that cyber-filmmakers still can't get perfect human expression *in* the eyes.

I also ask them to actually *direct* their actors — an obvious, but frequently necessary, request. So many directors assume that, simply by hiring a professional performer, the goods will be delivered. Invariably they will be, as most actors take pride in making this delivery whatever the circumstances. But how much more interesting and rewarding when the director mines beneath the obvious for hidden and unexpected riches.

Photography for the *G.Q.* article takes place in late December at Matt's office. Although an entire choice of Alexander's wardrobe hangs from a pipe there, I suggest giving the tuxedo and floppy bow yet another airing. The photographer, Frank Ockenfels, shoots several conventional portraits with a huge, old-fashioned camera that requires one to hold very still, as if posing for a daguerreotype. On one of the last rolls of film we decide to incorporate a borrowed prop, the huge Beast's claw that so menaced Michael Biehn on the mesa. It feels right — eye-catching and unpompous. I secretly hope that they choose this shot. (Later, by coincidence, a photographer friend calls from New York to say that he has seen the photos being processed in his lab and is encouragingly enthusiastic.)

I track down Brian in his bunker of an editing suite alongside John Lafferty, his affable, ponytailed editor, and their trusty Avid machine. This is the high-tech apotheosis of editing — no more scissors and white gloves with yards of film unspooling and spilling everywhere. They both claim to be pleased with the way it is all fitting together in an exotic blend of genres, now best described as *The Omen* meets *Air Force One* in *The End of Days* when they fight *The Battle of the Bulge.* This rough assembly is about two-and-a-half hours long and the whittling-down process continues. The Shakespeare quotes are still mostly intact, so the film remains, hopefully, a fusion of action and eloquence.

While there, I take the opportunity to add an approximation of the Beast's voice to the temporary sound track, another useful feature in the Avid's complex box of tricks, and I make an appointment to return in early January to do more. Finally vanity wins out. I ask Brian to show the scenes recorded just after my Italian dental drama to see if the tooth looks as strange as it felt. It doesn't: big smiles all round! I leave them to a supercharged schedule that allows only a brief two-day break for "The Holidays," as they are so carefully and ecumenically called here.

Pat and I decide not to endure another crowded flight and more unfamiliar accommodation and go to Hawaii for Christmas, as planned. Instead, we sit in our garden in paradisial weather, in prelapsarian bliss, guiltlessly reading books. The stress of the previous months falls from us like fruit from the tree of knowledge. At the Getty Museum an exquisite exhibition of Raphael drawings, many of a religious nature, revives joyful memories of our Italian sojourn, wafting a welcome breath of the Renaissance into our brave new western world.

There's also a sweet Christmas card from the Crouch family with a note reporting on their hectic, peripatetic year.

"Caylan can now give you a full dissertation about the difference between special effects and visual effects . . . while Cody can tell you where all the lizards are hiding on the set." Matt and Laurie conclude on a more solemn note, declaring a sense of awe and privilege at being allowed to re-envision Biblical truth for this generation using cinema. And, as Godard noted, in the cinema truth comes "twenty-four times a second."

CHAPTER ELEVEN

Re-arming

On the second day of the new year, 2001, I talk to Gary Bettman about our film's planned opening. Due to *Megiddo's* highly technical content, it won't be ready before late summer, and so the plan is to release it in a gap between other holiday blockbusters. Brian is still editing away and the film has slimmed down to 110 minutes. The cut footage includes scenes that proved redundant as they merely announced what was then seen happening. Gary promises to arrange for me to attend the first practical screening, probably in late March.

Meanwhile, on the twelfth of January, we meet at a studio to record the Beast's battlefield declamations. Rob Bredow sets up a video camera in front of me, as he did on the mesa, to also capture my mouth movements and facial expressions so they can be duplicated in the animation. The resulting footage must be as boring as that contradiction in terms, an Andy Warhol movie; but it's hard work — the voice has to pulse with power and energy to synthesize with Rob's first crude but impressive renderings of the Beast.

There is a system of "beeps" into a headphone that cue the exact beginning of a word or phrase. It demands concentration — and patience. When biorhythmically alert, I usually find this to be relatively straightforward. The hardest part comes when, reproducing the sound of vomiting wasps, I almost throw up again with the effort. My compensation is a bottle of beer labelled "Stone." Brewed in the San Diego area, it's label — unbelievably — has a Devil motif in its design.

It's now a time of year that I love. The Motion Picture Academy sends out a treasury of videos and DVDs of all the films that are potential Oscar contenders. Pat and I spend most evenings at home reviewing this pick of the crop on our behemoth of a TV with its upgraded sound system. The electronic dissemination of films has made for a more diverse, interesting, and less conservative choice, mitigating the fact that the ideal venue for viewing them should be the big screen.

In mid-January I'm interviewed by a Dominican priest for a book he is writing on religion in films. He astonishes me by claiming evidence of an "anti-Catholic bias" in *The Omega Code*. Requested to be specific, he cites the presence of a monstrance in Alexander's office, as well as regarding his nutrient wafers as "a mockery of transubstantiation." I can't believe that this was a subliminal, much less a deliberate intention.

It reminds me of other extraordinary things that have been read into films of mine. In Joseph Losey's *Accident* there was much earnest critical cerebration as to the significance of the dog that comes out of the house in the closing sequence. I was there when this long, end-credit sequence was filmed and witnessed the dog, bored like so many on a film set who, simply tired of waiting inside, ran out and, by pure chance, into the shot. Budget privations prevented any reshoot, thus engendering a cornucopia of intellectual pretentiousness.

Now that I'm home again, I can play a more active role as chairman of the California Youth Theatre. This organization, based on its British counterpart, of which I am a grateful graduate, has the same positive goals — to turn out better citizens by getting young people involved in the disciplines and passions of the performing arts. Drawing our members from every social and ethnic group in our melting pot of a city, we have just acquired and renovated a theater, the Ivar, in the entertainment capital of the world, Hollywood, as a Youth Arts Center.

In mid-February, I record a radio version of Chekhov's *The Sea Gull* and, playing the famed writer Trigorin, have eloquent insights into the nature of love, the creative life, and what it means to be a "celebrity." The latter has increasingly assumed a disproportionate status in America's free-for-all meritocracy, reminding me of a terse observation made by one of its own famed writers, John Updike: "Celebrity is a mask that eats into the face."

Nevertheless, it is in some measure on display when I lecture in Vancouver, the scene once again, because of the weak Canadian dollar, of so much Hollywood activity. In Los Angeles there are calls for this runaway production to be curtailed, but how can this be done when American moviemaking is essentially market-driven? Where will we go next, I wonder — India's thriving Bollywood?

My next port of call, though, is Miami where, again, strange things happen in my Florida hotel room. As I'm closing the curtains, their heavy rod falls from the wall, almost braining me. I'm removed in a hail of apologies to a vast, agoraphobic, Alexander-esque presidential suite whose previous occupant was indeed Bill Clinton.

I wonder if Clinton is now discovering the truth of Henry Kissinger's observation "Power is the ultimate aphrodisiac," a dictum that Stone so brazenly exemplifies. How must he feel about his successor who, within moments of taking over, was cynically tearing up campaign promises and world treaties with a gusto that made Alexander look like the model of political circumspection.

I'm also here, however, to attend a charity event on

behalf of the handicapped, which quickly puts into proper perspective all our petty problems.

One of the most delightful and unexpected outcomes of this trip is that I learn there is a portrait of me painted by Tennessee Williams. A photo of it is promised. On the return flight an attendant quizzes me for audition tips while another offers me a script she has written. I accept it — one of my happiest experiences resulted from a scenario sent equally out of the blue that turned out to be the film I made in Israel with Liv Ullmann, directed by the great cinematographer, Vilmos Zsigmond.

Back home, seasonal rains begin, and an insidiously leaking roof causes part of our kitchen ceiling to suddenly collapse, almost hitting Pat. Are these downfalls random or related?

The terror continues. It's now St. Valentine's Day, the anniversary of the occasion I proposed to Pat over three decades ago in Bombay, long before its name was mumbled into Mumbai. Somewhat perversely, we celebrate it by going to see Anthony Hopkins eating up the screen in *Hannibal*. Like *Megiddo*, the film was made both in Italy and the States and highlights a monster of excess being pursued by authority. I just hope our film swallows a similar healthy chunk of global revenue. I keep expecting Sir Tony to tear out someone's heart and, in commemoration of the day, gobble that down, too. Even Pat, whose cadaverous explorations have inured her to fleshly horrors, has to get up at one point for a stiff drink of water.

Matt has now moved his company into the old Hanna-Barbera studios. Its bright, cartoonish colors present a vivid contrast to his former gloomy, subterranean lair. Visiting, I find him hard at work at completing his other film, *Carmen the Champion,* for release in March of this year. A heart-warming story — or, "Rocky Meets God," in film-speak — it's part of Matt's new deal with the New York–based Good Times entertainment group. The intention is to produce films like *Megiddo,* that "don't violate the principles of faith," as compared to those with a more hard-hitting, hard-line spiritual message. Matt shows me a boxing sequence from *Carmen the Champion;* I just hope our "God vs. the Devil" rematch will be equally exciting, with knock-out blows at the box office. *Megiddo* is now down to a taut ninety-nine minutes; the effects, consuming 30 percent of the budget, will be ready in May. For the premier, live broadcasts are planned from forty-one different cities, spreading the word to the twenty-three million registered Christians who will no doubt constitute our core audience.

Pat and I set off again; I to speak at the LBJ library in Austin, Texas, while Pat has an exhibition of her photographs, a version of the one in Ghent, at the distinguished Corcoran Gallery of Art in Washington. We are discouraged from lingering on the East coast as, consistent with an apocalyptic meteorological trend, the city is about to be scoured and cleansed by the most massive snowstorm to hit since 1898. Across the Atlantic, my rain-sodden native land is suffering from its own fiendish woes. On top of the mad cow malady, foot-and-mouth disease is spreading; as one doom-laden headline bewails, "In Britain, the Isle of Contagion, one virus brings the medieval into modern life."

In other journalistic news, Matt tells me that we are now promoted to being the lead story in the *G.Q.* Among other publishing tie-ins, there will be a "novelization" of the screenplay. Meanwhile, he invites me on an informal TBN live broadcast with Laurie. As well as reminiscing about the experience of making *Megiddo,* we talk about the modern-dress Christian mythology that is its essence.

This is also discussed in the March *G.Q.* magazine — "The Hollywood Issue" — which sells out soon after arriving on the newsstands. Amidst the Babylon of advertisements, the Sodom of smiles and the Gomorrah of narcissism, the superstars and wannabes, we are heavily featured under the headline, "God is on line one." "For years fundamentalist Christians avoided Hollywood like the plague," a subtitle reads, "but times have changed — times have become biblically ripe." A portrait of Matt looking intensely charismatic fills one entire page. "The Antichrist is ready for his close-up," the article begins, and indeed, there's also a photo of myself looking bemused through my devil's claw. I *knew* they would use this unusual shot, and I'm glad they did!

There's a further opportunity to meditate on our film's theme of faith, power, and loyalty when Pat and I attend the Los Angeles Opera's production of Handel's *Giulio Cesare.* At the performance, I encounter Stephen Hawking who I haven't seen since our student days at University when he coxed the college rowing team. With a most un-English forwardness, I seize the opportunity to thank him for all he has done since those days to similarly guide our imaginations to new frontiers.

The opera's villain Tolomeo, I'm pleased to note, also wears Stone's long coat and, during the military episodes, is even bold enough to carry my wished-for fly whisk. The opera is a showcase for the unearthly beauty of the counter-tenor voice, especially that of David Daniels who sings the title role. I had met him in a TV studio on my Vancouver trip and promised to attend. The haunting beauty of the four-hour performance stays with us for days, exemplifying the truthfulness of the observation that Bach — like Handel — is proof of the existence of God.

But meeting up with David afterward, we witnessed the human cost behind the sublime facade. Mold in his hotel room had affected his voice, reminding one how fragile the performer's art is, and what strength it requires, and how unfrivolous the artist's demands for congenial accommodation and travel. I shall always remember meeting Rudolph Nureyev, also backstage in his dressing room, and witnessing the devilish punishment that a lifetime of ballet had inflicted on his feet.

Meanwhile, there's punishment for Europe too as the plague spreads to France. In Britain there are rumors of vigilante squads being organized to prevent distraught farmers from killing, not their cattle, but themselves. Black smoke from the pyres of burning carcasses pollutes the once green and pleasant land, hovering over the fields like our bombs exploding over Megiddo.

The election of Britain's next Prime Minister is delayed and in LA we meet up again with a former one, John Major, here on another speaking tour. He asks us to an enjoyable, impromptu dinner, and the next morning, St. Patrick's Day, we invite him back for tea and then to an Irish party. John, however, the personification of dedication, remains immured in his hotel room writing. No doubt he was thereby proving that his pen was mightier than any sword, however scrupulously wielded, militarily or politically.

In late March there is another ADR "looping" session. I drive to the Vine Street studios warming up my voice with exercises en route, knowing how vocally demanding my

Beast can be. (We do strange things in our cars here: I have long urged Pat to do a photo essay on women drivers making up in car mirrors while stopped!) I have also brought Throat Coat tea to soothe and lubricate, and something edible to discourage involuntary mid-morning tummy rumbles that register on the sound track like so many atomic explosions.

The session goes smoothly. Brian has moved the "I have been here before" speech with Udo at Megiddo to the very beginning of the film. Preceding even the opening titles, it feels right there, setting the tone and parameters of the ensuing conflict perfectly. The satanic voice recorded at the previous session seems too forced and, like that fat boy in Dickens, too self-consciously "horrific." I decide to make it more natural, trusting in the sound technicians' wizardry to later boost it with roars and reverberations into something not of this world.

During Oscar week I meet up again with Jack Cardiff, who is here to receive an Academy Award for his now legendary contribution to the medium as a cinematographer. We discuss further *One Life Later,* the film he is going to direct with myself in a leading role. Like *Megiddo,* it has a spiritual underpinning and is equally ambitious. In his patched tweed jacket and tie, Jack brings a whiff of a traditional, vanishing Britain into the upstart, trendy purlieus of Hollywood. Sitting by his hotel pool, we work on the script. Despite jet lag and advanced years — Jack is now eighty-six — he radiates an infectious enthusiasm, telling me that last night he had been energized by speaking to a class of young people at a screening of his magnificently photographed *A Matter of Life and Death.* I only wish I could have half of his creative, dynamic *joie de vivre* when I'm his age.

It reminds me of telephoning Sir John Gielgud on his ninety-sixth birthday last year and enquiring how he had celebrated it, expecting him to say that, like Justice Shallow, he had sat musing in his garden. "Oh, I've been filming all day," he enthused, "Samuel Beckett!" John has left us a painting in his will — a potent reminder of a great and gracious life, a good friend, and exemplary role model. We also recently attended a ninetieth birthday party for the distinguished film director, Ronald Neame, who reported that the doctors who ordered him to give up smoking are all long since dead! The active longevity of all three men seems to perfectly illustrate the sagacity of George Burns' best advice — "to fall in love with what you do for a living."

Fortunately my profession prefers its member to stay in the race for the long run, even if they are not all winners and are frequently left behind. To expect to do "significant" work every time one bursts out of the starting blocks, when the curtain rises or "action!" is requested, is unrealistic. For the most part, we provide entertainment — an honorable undertaking. Just occasionally, however, the opportunity presents itself to be involved in something that shapes or re-defines public opinion and taste — and that is truly rewarding.

Pat must have felt this way when, at her opening at the Corcoran in Washington, its Curator of Photography, Philip Brookman, revealed in a speech that after years of being involved in the medium, Pat's photographs had had a profound effect on him, causing him to re-examine such issues as life and death in a fundamental new way. The gallery has acquired all of her works they exhibited for its permanent collection.

Jack is luminous on the Oscar show, which gives him that elusive, essential Hollywood property, "heat." I'm now hopeful that *One Life Later* will be in production around the time that *Megiddo* is released. Speculation about the latter being considered for awards next year — perhaps for its special effects — flit idly through my imagination.

Meanwhile in April, it's back to work in the shape of a television pilot filmed at Universal Studios. It's fun to be inside a big studio again. Universal is like a giant queen bee — or is it wasp? — attended by thousands of busy workers.

Matt's rainbow'd office is adjacent and is equally hectic when I drop by. Adding to the temporary track, I improvise a sardonic *touché* as Michael Biehn is clubbed down when coming to confront me before the battle. Peter Bernstein, who will compose *Megiddo*'s score, is introduced, as is Glenn Morgan who will supervise the final "mix" when, hopefully, all the elements will come together. Matt tells me that the general release of the film has now been postponed until late September — giving everyone a much appreciated breathing space.

CHAPTER TWELVE

Trench Warfare

On the twelfth of April there's finally a chance to see *Megiddo's* first cut. I'm positively impressed both with the edited narrative and the preliminary rendering of the visual effects. As well as creating some loathsome demons, Rob Bredow has filled the battlefield skies with streaking jets and helicopters, while the first digital manifestations of the huge, contending armies of troops and tanks take sinister shape. The "fatal handshake" now actually shows Stone's malignancy flowing like a poison through the arteries and veins of the US president to his heart.

"I would like to congratulate all those involved in putting the film together so far," my producer's notes begin. "It makes the most powerful statement, and is entertaining without being preachy. I'm glad that I haven't seen the cut for some time, because I came to it relatively fresh and with a heightened objectivity."

The most important note concerns a scene I consider one of the key "beats" in the film. "This is the controversial moment where Stone vomits the wasps that provoke the Chinese into action. I notice that the accompanying "ceremony" with the Guardian has been cut. I think it should be restored — or at least some of it. This is a major transformative scene in which Stone manifests as "The Beast," but still in human form. From this moment on people refer to him as such, so it's important to make something of its incarnation. In a sense, the scene is a reprise of the "ceremony" where young Stone is initiated demonically. I think we should present anew the elements that played there — the Latin Black Mass, the computer-generated demons, and also the image of the Guardian in his monkish cowl. All these added features will help provoke and justify Gabriella's swift descent into madness (so it's not just the wasps that tip her over the edge)."

Amongst the material edited out there is nothing I really miss, although I'm chagrined to see that, yet again, my violin playing has not survived the cut! There's a quick response from Brian — or as he puts it, "To the Beast; from the cage cleaner" — in general agreeing with my comments, and now awaiting the reaction of our associate producers.

Literary matters dominate LA in the meantime. There's a Festival of Books — the largest on the planet — exemplifying the astonishing fact (for smug New Yorkers, at least) that people buy more books in this city than anywhere else in America. (Whether they read them is another matter, as many in our industry hire their own "readers.")

I'm happy to see that our Shakespeare book is among those featured, and I'm invited to discuss the Bard on a panel that includes Marc Norman, the co-writer with Tom Stoppard of one of my favorites among recent films, *Shakespeare in Love*. I compliment Marc on his movie's "multi-level" experience, a quality it shares with Shakespeare's plays that appeals to both ignoramus and intellectual alike.

I also host a tribute to our Mayor, Richard Riordan, a great champion of literacy, who is about to retire. Among those who join me on stage are Haley Joel Osment and Jamie Lee Curtis who delight the audience in a time-honored activity still fundamental to the movies — telling a story. (Pat and I belong to the Mayor and his wife, Nancy's, book club and relish the monthly discussion of a literary work over dinner. Equally enjoyable is the inevitable political conversation that ensues.) I'm also pleased to run into William Nolan, the author of *Logan's Run,* and we speculate on rumors now circulating that our film is about to be remade. Perhaps I could now play that representative of a wrinklier generation, the Peter Ustinov character.

It's Shakespeare, though, who runs off with my imagination when, in May, I'm asked to present him in two programs with the National Symphony Orchestra conducted by Leonard Slatkin, at Washington's Kennedy Center. The first is the thrilling William Walton/ *Henry V* collaboration from Olivier's great film; the second is a program of Shakespeare poetry that I've compiled to go with music inspired by him. Performing them proves to be as soul-stirring as it is nerve-wracking, especially the latter program that is only briefly rehearsed. However, when the synergy between words and music sparks, something remarkable happens — that rare and awesome moment "when the gods speak."

Certainly Matt is aiming for similar divine, and even musical, intervention. He informs me that *Megiddo* will now have its premiere on Rosh Hashanah, the Jewish "Feast of Trumpets," on September eighteenth. There will be a live telecast from the Mount of Olives that, in duplication of our film's finale, will perhaps record the promised return of the Deity to earth in a panoply of white light and celestial trumpeting.

In mid-May, Pat and I fly off to a Europe where the media mogul, Silvio Berlusconi, has just been elected to run Italy. What are the chances that he, too, will soon be making a rabble-rousing speech outside the Colosseum? We are to visit London, Warsaw, Budapest, and Lisbon, all in two fleeting weeks!

The weather is perfect. Flying into London, Leonardo's former assistant is thrilled to be again invited into the cockpit to marvel at the sunlit, sea-girt counties unfolding below.

Our arrival at the Ritz coincides with the hotel's ninety-fifth birthday and we're invited to the celebrations. Again, the culture shock of the English *en fête* is immediate, but there are enough old friends on hand to soften the blow.

Across Piccadilly at the Royal Academy another exhibition has depictions of Hell, but this time exquisite ones. Botticelli's illustrations for Dante's *Divine Comedy* have been collected together for the first time in centuries. Even those suffering the torments of the damned are depicted with the most delicate touch writhing in aesthetic agony. There's a wonderful illustration, too, of a furry, be-winged beast.

Revisiting my parents I'm relieved to find they are adapting to my father's invalidism. I chat with my mother in the leafy Sussex garden that she herself still proudly tends. My father, a decorated combatant in what was assumed to be the world's final conflict, as well as someone who once studied to be a priest, expresses interest in reading these pages.

I also take part in a filmed tribute to Dirk Bogarde. My screen tutor in *Accident* when I was learning his trade, Dirk taught me screen acting at its most subtle and refined. I'm pleased to note, though, that he also played his own extro-vert monster of depravity in Visconti's *The Damned*.

Camilla Parker-Bowles comes into soft focus again at a country dinner party, but there's little chance to talk, let alone dance. It feels odd to be back in a forelock-tugging culture after so much free-wheeling egalitarianism State-side. It reminds me of the memorable phrase that Paul Ther-oux used about the English — that they are guilty of "condescending envy"! Besides, constitutional monarchy appears so quaint and toothless to me after having wielded Alexander's totalitarian powers.

Warsaw seems still stunned by its satanic near-annihilation by another beast. In a vast mausoleum of a the-ater, we participate in a televised film awards show. Pat and I also find time to visit the Zahenta Gallery where she had a recent photographic show. I learn that I was part of a con-troversial exhibit there, featuring photos of actors playing Nazis. The ludicrous notion was implied that, by accept-ing such roles, the performers endorsed their characters' phi-losophy and behavior. How should that make me feel about playing the Devil!

The Polish actor Daniel Olbrychski, with whom I once literally crossed swords in the epic *The Secret of the Sahara,* took it upon himself to avenge scorned thespian honor. Dramatically unfurling a sword from his coat, he slashed out the portraits of himself and such other neo-Nazis as Alain Delon, Jean-Paul Belmondo, and, I'm delighted to say, Michael York.

But there are pleasures here, too — not least the local asparagus that is in mouth-watering seasonal perfection.

In Hungary, I'm the on-camera host of a new TV pilot for a proposed series on philosophy. It's filmed, for reasons too abstruse to explain now, on a raft in the middle of Lake Balaton. We're happy to be back in this country, the location of so many enjoyable film experiences, having had the pleasure of witnessing it turn — like the Czech Republic and Croatia — from dispirited Communist drabness to vibrant capitalist chic.

Our first visit in the early 1980s set the tone. Driving our car up through Yugoslavia, we arrived at a frontier bristling with barbed wire and beset with watchtowers where our papers were lengthily examined by the armed guards surrounding us. As unease and irrational guilt began to set in, one of them pulled out a paper of his own from under his greatcoat, smiled and asked for an autograph, wishing us both welcome.

Next, Lisbon and the delightful Troia Film Festival in Setubal, reached across an exhilarating string of bridges spanning the Tagus like the wind-swollen sails on the galleons that once so enriched the country. There we encounter the actress Florinda Bolkan, an old friend and this year's jury president. Florinda astonishes Pat and myself by revealing that she has an Italian villa — in, of all places, Bracciano — that we would have been welcome to use during the shooting!

After this brief encounter with Portuguese culture and, particularly, a succession of meals enhanced by the delicious local rice, we head home. I'm bearing another welcome accolade, the Golden Dolphin, and have also been honored with a little plaque in the local cinema alongside Lauren Bacall, with whom I once happily committed murder wearing that *Orient Express* overcoat. Lauren and I were also fellow guests at one of the most congenial film festivals of all:

Cognac, in France. Here the shortage of hotels assures that guests are put up either chez Hennessy, Camus, or Rémy-Martin! *Santé!*

On the flight back I'm returned to murderous mood, encountering new horror in the form of vomited words, not wasps. Involuntarily, we are made to listen to a Hollywood casting director yelling on the phone, at ten dollars a minute, in a tone that penetrates both earplugs and head-phones for the entire eleven-hour trip. Now I know why some film budgets are so top-heavy. Perhaps I should adopt his nerve-shredding voice as the Beast's, especially as it's now early June and I'm due to "loop" all that needs to be done, sound-wise, to my role before the film is finally mixed.

Before this crucial ADR session in early June, I ask to review the final cut, scrutinizing it repeatedly until I have a clear idea of what changes can, and need to, be made. Some are obvious and routine — such as indistinct dialogue that requires clarification.

There's one scene, however, that I would like to entirely re-voice with different words and intonation. It's where Stone returns from Africa and meets Gabriella, herself just back from ministering to the sick and dying in Mexico. Originally positioned earlier in the film, the sequence now comes *after* the wasp episode that initiates Stone's beastly transformation. As a result, my behavior seems wrong: It's almost friendly where it should be menacing and malevolent. Kissing Gabriella here weakens Stone's previous powerful dismissal of her, particularly as I've managed to insert a looped "You've lost my love" into that moment to help provoke and justify her ensuing swift descent into madness.

John, the editor, and Glenn Morgan, the post-production supervisor, are in agreement. Brian is away in Canada filming another movie, but I feel I now know his intentions well enough not to betray him. Matt has given me a free hand to make whatever changes seem appropriate. Fortunately much of this scene was played on my back and we re-voice it so that the dialogue is harder and crueller. The kiss becomes a mocking, ironic "well done" — each word dropped into her ears like poison.

Elsewhere we add further flourishes. My unused "go to hell" is finally worked in as I hurl my father to his death and, kneeling in the courtyard over his body, I manage to transform my feigned sobs into more audible laughter. This is carried over the cut into the following "coronation" scene with Udo on the Temple Mount. During the great battle of Armageddon I add some more dialogue for Satan to thunder as the conflict rages around him. It's too expensive — and too late — to actually see more of me, but I'm hopeful that my disembodied voice will provide a continuous, terrifying presence. It's exhilarating to have this technical gift that enables one to mend and emend and, hopefully, gild the lily.

Some of the special effects are still not finished, so we agree to return for a final session when they are ready. The day has been long and exhausting and my thanks are sincere and inadequate for all that the technicians have done to make such significant changes possible.

CHAPTER THIRTEEN

Countdown to Armageddon

The Producers becomes a smash hit on Broadway, turning the substance of the Holocaust into showbiz hilarity. Real, as opposed to staged, evil is encountered when Timothy McVeigh, the modern incarnation of malevolence, is painlessly put to a sanitized death. His "celebrity" status is confirmed with his every thought and moment being given the same unremittingly intense scrutiny accorded our showbiz and sports idols. His end is even broadcast and recorded by a rapt press. What's next . . . "Snuff" TV?

But we're cheated of any deathbed confession. Even more unrepentant than our film's Satan, McVeigh leaves us not with Alexandrine bravura, but with bathos from a minor poet, confirming the famous association of evil with banality. There's one ray of civilized hope, though. Slobodan Milosevic, who commandeered headlines so ruthlessly during the composition of this diary, is indicted for war crimes by the United Nations Tribunal in The Hague, and his extradition and trial requested.

There's optimism, too, on the professional front. The threatened Writers' Guild strike is settled, making the resolution of the upcoming Actors' strike more likely, particularly in the present uneasy economic climate. The dam holding film projects in abeyance, pending the satisfactory outcome of negotiations, should now begin to crumble. Meanwhile, on the writing front, I'm pleased to learn that these dispatches will be published as a book, together with photos from the battlefront.

Matt, still waiting for those special effects, announces a further delay until July 9th. Then all the filmic elements will start to be "mixed," the end result, hopefully, being greater than the sum of its disparate parts. At the end of June, I make the pilgrimage down to TBN's headquarters in Costa Mesa to bear witness at another live broadcast. Trinity Christian City International appears like a gleaming mirage amidst the surrounding unremarkable acres of freeway-bound development. Set within gardens and reflecting pools, it's a palatial amalgam of high-tech and highbrow.

There are reunions with the Crouch family — not only Matt, Laurie, and the boys, but also with Paul and his gracious wife, Jan, who have just played host to a Chinese delegation. Shown parts of the film, these "Kings of the East" were apparently intrigued to learn that their countrymen are to play such starring roles in the world's great denouement!

In a studio illuminated by stained glass windows that glint off the gold-leafed furniture and pews, a respectful audience is seated. Marilyn McCoo and Billy Davis Jr. get the broadcast off to a lively start with some rousing gospel music. Then Gil Colon joins me for the on-camera interview. A trailer of *Megiddo* is shown, and Matt surprises me by reading some excerpts from this diary. I'm a little concerned, as neither film nor book is properly finished, but I sense that we are now at the start of an aggressive advertising campaign that will only intensify. "In the beginning was the word," and the word is unmistakably upbeat. I learn that to spread it, Matt is about to embark on a tour of American cities.

Independence Day is spent celebrating, not so much the old Revolution, but the new resolution of the threatened actors' strike, even though such contentious questions as Internet compensation are barely addressed. We lunch at a fellow Brit's house where our independence is perversely asserted with gastronomic fireworks in the form of blazing hot curries, quenched by the sort of strong tea that was so provocatively dumped in Boston harbor. The anniversary of the end of British tyranny also happens to be the day that our token contemporary tyrant, Slobodan Milosevic, is hauled before the World Court.

Two days later I find myself back in the recording studio for that final session. This time Brian is able to join us, and both his input and benign company are welcome. Settling a sneaking doubt, he confirms that our guessed pronunciation, Meg*eed*o, is in fact the correct Hebrew, although I suspect that common usage will prefer a more "Armag*ed*don"-like sound. Brian also reports on the positive progress of Peter Bernstein's musical score. Working with a synthesizer, Peter has apparently created a menacing leitmotif to accompany Stone.

As a warm-up to the ensuing beastly braying, we re-voice the opening biblical quotation, the timing of its phrases having been altered. Depicting the Beast was a huge demand on Rob Bredow and his visual effects team; but they have performed wonders. Their rendition of the Antichrist, although not yet quite pixel-perfect, is already frightening and real. His form has now been literally fleshed out on a skeleton that is eerily reversed, with vertebrae to the front. The animating of the molten lava that will flow in the veins of this hideous creature remains to be done.

I find that there is just room enough to add "the Beast" to the "Lucifer," "Beelzebub," and other satanic names accompanying Stone's battlefield transformation, declaimed just as this is completed. We next record some suitable cries of despairing agony as Satan is returned to Hell, finding himself now chained to the Fiery Lake "that he should deceive the nations no more, till the thousand years should be fulfilled."

The vomiting of the wasps is revocalized. This time I find the best effect is achieved by yelling with a mouth full of liquid into the studio trash can! By midday we are finished and I make plans to join Glenn Morgan at the mix that begins next week when, God willing, the Trinity of Narrative, Effects, and Score will finally coalesce into One.

Meanwhile, an amusing fax arrives from Adrian Brine who, in his self-appointed role as Don Adriano ("a Pedant" among the myriad minor players in Shakespeare's canon) offered to give these pages a preliminary critical appraisal: "Just read *Armageddon* on the Amsterdam-Paris TGV. I was sitting opposite a sinister foreign gent (out of Graham Greene) while reading you on Slobodan Milosevic. 'Excuse me, is this The Hague? Where they lock up so-called war criminals?' he enquired. 'The International Court's here, yes,' I replied. He laughed merrily: 'International? Kha-kha (was he Russian? — that's how they laugh in Turgenev)

'*Real* war criminals are elsewhere!' he confided, and before I could say Saddam, he whispered, (stage whisper) 'Washington!!' and more glottal laughter. I put up your manuscript as a barrier against further insights."

Faxing back thanks, I'm also pleased to tell Adrian that our Shakespeare book is a finalist in the 2001 Independent Publisher Book Awards. Mention of Greene reminds me that a 1972 film of his *England Made Me,* in which I participated, and of which he personally expressed approval, will be screened at this year's Graham Greene Festival in Berkhamsted, England. Set in Nazi Germany, it features a ruthless, Alexander-type industrialist, played by Peter Finch, who is "beaten unless he has the world." The only discordant note is that, apparently, a print of the film has been hard to locate. It seems incredible that a successful piece of cinema should so swiftly be in danger of becoming as ephemeral as a stage performance.

More welcome news comes in the form of an Emmy nomination for my sozzled swashbuckler in AMC's *The Lot.* The true prize, though, remains our film that, with its now imminent release, begins to loom on the horizon like a monstrous whirlwind thundering toward us.

I drop by the Burbank studio where the "pre-dubbing" is in progress. This is a laborious process where dialogue is made clear and consistent before the mix, even if this requires poaching the odd syllable from elsewhere. John, the editor, and Glenn, the post-production supervisor, report continued positive progress.

"Jesus Rocks!" is the huge headline on the cover of *Newsweek* magazine's July 16th edition. Over a picture of some deliriously happy young people, a more restrained subtitle declares: "Christian entertainment makes a joyful noise." According to this publication, *Megiddo* is part of "A Holy Phenom," an explosion of faith-based culture that even includes a Christian Wrestling Federation.

"Can a movement become a mass market without selling its soul?" the magazine enquires, and invites Matt's comment. "'Hollywood was considered Sodom and Gomorrah,' says Crouch, who keeps a Bible on his desk next to those industry bibles: *Variety* and *The Hollywood Reporter*. 'I truly believe that once the Christian community understands that they have a vote by buying a ticket, they will become the country's largest single market.'"

This is perhaps necessary, as the same article asserts that movies represent "the one category in which a Christian product has yet to make a major splash," yet adding in reference to that earlier Holy Phenom, and (in perverse contradiction), "though 1999's *The Omega Code* shocked Hollywood by opening in the box-office top ten." Matt, while not selling his soul or even wrestling with it, certainly commits to selling his movie, embarking on an evangelical twenty-city tour to announce the advent of *Megiddo*.

Concurrently, the first release is issued by Howard Brandy, the publicist hired to officially promote our film. "*Megiddo* is a cautionary tale," he writes, "a broad depiction of the Antichrist, his rise to power and the ensuing climactic battle between the Titans of good and evil told on an epic scale. On another level, it is also a rousing adventure film with supernatural, fantasy, and religious overtones. The filmmakers learned with *The Omega Code* what the audience wanted and now they are delivering it in a way that will be more impactful than the first movie." "There is no way," Matt is quoted as saying, "to have the armies of the world in one shot. It's impossible. But we do!"

Beijing is announced as the venue for the next Olympic Games. I'm delighted that my wasp-incited Armageddon allies are being rewarded. It's timely news for Pat, too, as she's in the midst of preparing a huge photographic exhibition for China in November of this year. Perversely, I hope that I'm out of work then, and thus able to accompany her to a country that neither of us has visited.

On the domestic artistic front, a photo arrives of my charming portrait painted around the time of *Outcry* by Tennessee Williams: "The kindness of strangers," indeed. There's also an invitation to be the guest of honor at the Breckenridge Film Festival in the Rocky Mountains the week before *Megiddo* is released on September 21st. I conspire with Matt to get a print of the film screened there. The timing — not to mention the publicity — is perfect.

Marilyn McCoo and Billy Davis Jr. are again encountered at a lavish Hollywood party where they are entertaining alongside such other legends as Stevie Wonder, Barry Manilow, Coolio, and — good golly, Miss Molly — my own teenage favorite, Little Richard. Pat Boone, another entertainer evangelist, also sings. He's seated at our table where we talk about the significance of *The Omega Code* and the expectations for its sequel.

In mid-July Pat and I fly to New York, mostly dozing en route. The previous night, while I updated this text, Pat completed preparations for yet another photographic exhibition, this one opening in Santa Fe, New Mexico, in early August. But Manhattan exerts its usual instant energizing. While Pat raids the galleries and museums, I take part in a photo shoot for the *New York Times*. The pictures will appear in its Sunday magazine the same week that *Megiddo* is released, so I regard this as another potential weapon in our film's publicity armory.

We also go to see *The Producers* — and laugh from start to finish. There is only one chilling moment in this zany, gay (in every sense) extravaganza when a chorus of Nazi storm troopers marches in a swastika formation, jolting disturbing memories of the Chapman brothers' frightening *Apocalypse* display in London.

Perhaps I'm being oversensitive about this issue. I think

back to the time I was on Broadway in *Bent,* a play with a Holocaust setting that also dealt with issues of homosexuality, a Nazi crime punished in their death camps. One night a young girl came to see me backstage, telling me that her mother, a real concentration camp internee, had also been at the performance to witness the reenactment of the unspeakable horrors she had experienced. Thinking I was about to be censured for perhaps trivializing her mother's experience into entertainment, I was astonished when the girl thanked me. She explained how the play had acted as a catalyst so that, for the first time, her mother had been able to speak about what had happened. The drama had manifested in its ancient spiritual form, as a potent psychic healer. I was infinitely moved.

Again we run into Julie Taymor and her husband, Elliot, in the happy crowd exiting the theater, some even blithely chorusing *Springtime for Hitler.* Over drinks at Joe Allen's, Julie tells us that she is also in post-production on another film with a huge and complex personality in its title role. This one is about Frida Kahlo and, even though Julie is now an established and distinguished film director — one for whom significant actors are prepared to play small roles, she is just hoping that the film's intense political content will survive the process intact. I only hope that we can finally collaborate on a project that will take wing and fly.

I have been invited to lecture in, of all delightful places, Martha's Vineyard, the sandy spit of an island off the far Massachusetts coast and a world away from the frantic pace of the Big Apple. This is the summer home of a power elite with whom Stone Alexander would feel comfortably at home in his blazer and Nantucket red trousers. I see his confident ghost strutting and ingratiating amidst their luxurious yachts and villas while private jets streak in from the bastions of industry and influence.

The weather is picture-postcard perfect, but I resist both its siren call and the charms of this seductive spot in order to attempt to conclude this narrative. It can never be finished in a conventional sense, with an epilogue or even an unequivocal "The End" because, if this publication is to coincide with the film's release ("a consummation devoutly to be wished"), I must begin to curtail these jottings *in media res.*

I call Los Angeles for the latest word on our post-production. Both John and Glenn again sound optimistic when I interrupt them in the studio. The dialogue pre-dubs have been finished and those for the effects are progressing well — I can hear them booming and crashing in the background as we speak.

The mix of the six reels that constitute our movie will be finished only by the second week of August, so that the film for the premiere will probably arrive still dripping wet from the lab! Matt is in the middle of his twenty-city tour and reports a huge interest in what started out as his "apocalyptic kind of thing." This time 10,000 Prayer Warriors have volunteered to proclaim the word that is already being disseminated at a web site displaying *Megiddo*'s devilish horned M logo.

Pat and I next head to Washington where I'm to give a Shakespeare lecture at the Corcoran, winding up a year of speaking engagements. As the plane lands at the airport renamed to honor President Reagan, I glimpse the White House where its present incumbent labors at the realization of the Gipper's Star Wars missile shield. Designed to preserve this Home of the Brave from a surprise Armageddon, will it prove adequate against wasps?

I worry that Americans, the present superstar victors on the bloody playing field of history, will now abandon "the greatness thrust upon them" and, in pursuit of narrow nationalist goals, fudge their country's inevitable role as the world's moral leader. I'm glad that *Megiddo,* at least, is unambiguous in its moral values.

Back in LA I read a news report of a pitched battle on Jerusalem's Temple Mount. My end is my beginning. "For he who controls Jerusalem at the Last Days. . . "

Santa Fe comes and goes, and Pat enjoys another success. Among her more recent studies of cadavers and nudes, I'm pleased to see that the gallery has selected others, taken on our three decades of film travels. Enlarged to a dramatic size, there are tribesmen in Marrakech, holy men in India, and other subjects so singularly captured as to personify Proust's observation that "The real voyage of discovery consists, not in seeing new landscapes, but in having new eyes." I hope there will be further opportunities to similarly relive other film locations we have shared. Images of Italy, Ireland,

Germany, Holland, and Japan merge with others from Spain, France, Jamaica, and Hungary, blending with still more from Brazil, Tunisia, Norway, and Australia. A keen desire is also provoked, especially here in Georgia O'Keeffe country, to see more of these United and very photogenic States.

"There is a tide in the affairs of men," Shakespeare's Brutus observes, "which, taken at the flood, leads on to fortune." In early August, I sense this tide beginning to rise — and in the mainstream, too — when Bill Maher invites me on his irreverent late night TV show, *Politically Incorrect*. One of the topics is prompted by that recent *Newsweek* article about Christian entertainment in which Matt and *Megiddo* were profiled.

"Is there a new demand for family values from Hollywood?" Bill asks in his inimitable, cynically amused way. Fellow guests include Garry Marshall, the veteran producer and director, who has just found more box-office fortune with his G-rated, family-oriented film, *The Princess Diaries*. "G used to stand for G-spot" Garry jokes, and I'm about to respond that it could now stand for God when Kristi

Hamrick from the Washington-based Family Research Council refers to *The Omega Code* and its huge success. This is my cue and — there's no polite holding back or waiting for one's turn on this raucous show — I jump in. Against Bill's devil's-advocate protestations, I insist that the film's success was not an aberration but a clear indication of a popular trend. I manage to mention *Megiddo* before the conversation lurches onto such other "hot-button" issues as cloning and the present First Lady.

A former president is in the news, too. Riding back in the limo, I read that Bill Clinton will receive a record $10 million for his memoirs — the entire budget of a modest film. I speculate on how many books will need to be sold in order to recoup such an investment, particularly if its text reflects this current return to family values, and the name Lewinsky is not to be found in its index!

Inevitably, there will be critical appraisal to face — as with the movies. Another film this year about a major climactic battle, *Pearl Harbor,* has already been dismissed with faint praise, despite earning enough millions as to make Clinton's fee look paltry. Critics are "the firing squad that waits in every city," according to Tennessee Williams. But I want no blindfold or last cigarette. I honestly feel that I have given *my* best shot to *Megiddo* and so can face our shared destiny with a certain equanimity. Of course I would prefer the film to be successful. Meritocratic America relates more comfortably to winners than to losers, for whom the deepest scorn is reserved.

A well-aimed critical fusillade can be useful and at least kills cleanly, sparing one lingering agonies. So many, though, merely maim or are wildly off the mark, producing just noise and smoke. Irresponsible critics should be warned that, on the seventh level of Dante's *Inferno,* such Sowers of Discord are condemned to reap an especially ghastly eternal punishment!

I know that, however *Megiddo* turns out or is received, it will have a special place in my ever-lengthening résumé. Making it was both enriching and rewarding — qualities I hope that will be shared by its audience. In a few weeks, it will join a myriad of other films "out there" in the vast, ever-expanding universe of moving images.

I would like to think that there will be other movies

ahead — already the toothy, bespectacled spectre of Austin Powers has leeringly reappeared, inviting me to leap from the sublime to the ridiculous, from the Beast to Basil, and join him in a third outrageous outing this fall. Will the third edition of *The Omega Code* ever become more than just a dream? What a bizarre profession I practice! The cards remain permanently unstacked, the playing fields flatly even, and the Holy Grail of guaranteed success ever elusive.

In late August, the headlines are full of stories about the crisis in Macedonia. By now, even that check-in agent at the Los Angeles airport should know about this country's existence. I shall be forever grateful that the movies have enabled Pat and myself to obtain insights more immediate and compelling than any newspaper or newsreel could provide. I talk to Matt who is just back from Europe arranging the film's overseas premieres. The Rosh Hashanah trumpets will sound three times to herald *Megiddo* in Jerusalem, Rome, and Los Angeles. Meanwhile, there's a din of instruments busily tuning up.

The fate of our complex, costly, and creative enterprise that will soon be revealed to "Th' yet unknowing world," is once more in the hands of the aforementioned Divinity who, like the most benign and creative film editor, "shapes our ends, rough-hew them how we will." Certainly after so much preparation, dedication, and anticipation — to borrow yet another phrase from Hamlet, someone who so valued the actor and his art — "The readiness is all."

August 20, 2001

EPILOGUE

On Sunday, September 9th a mild earthquake rocked Los Angeles, setting the pattern for a week in which the world would be jolted to its foundations. On Monday morning this book was sent off to be published. The very next day, September 11th, a foretaste of Armageddon was visited on the United States when four of its airliners, flush with fuel and filled with innocent passengers, were hijacked and transformed into guided weapons of mass destruction. Those symbols of America's financial and military might, New York's twin-towered World Trade Center and Washington's Pentagon, became terrorist targets, with catastrophic loss of life and property. A massive blow was also dealt to America's sense of invulnerability.

"The readiness is all," I had noted in the last line of the preceding diary, but no one could have anticipated this extraordinary eventuality. A numbed, shocked disbelief mingled with outrage set in. Life seemed to be put on hold. Regular broadcasting was scrapped, the scenes of devastation and the heroic rescue efforts becoming a round-the-clock staple. It was repeatedly observed that the oft-replayed fiery explosions and collapse of the towers in a pall of smoke and dust "looked just like the movies." Indeed, many of the television images were disturbingly reminiscent of some of the more heart-stopping special effects in *Megiddo.* I only wished that it was now simply a question of flicking a switch on an editing machine to have the whole horrific sequence reversed and the cityscape restored to what it had so proudly been.

The following day, Hollywood reacted by postponing or canceling films that had themes of terror and violence. On Thursday the 13th I met with several of *Megiddo's* production, promotion, and marketing executives in Matt's office to discuss the appropriateness of releasing our film in this changed climate. I counseled delaying until the smoke, both literally and figuratively, had had a chance to clear. Also, the impending Los Angeles premiere, with its klieg lights and red carpet, should now be turned into a candlelit prayer vigil, something that TBN was eminently qualified to facilitate.

Others more closely affiliated with the network saw the

film as providentially placed to provide a message of healing and inspiration, and they urged its immediate release. Although their sincerity was undoubted, I sensed that this was not the time for the display of anything that risked being interpreted as extremism. Again, as someone outside "the family," I felt I could best represent all those who did not share their degree of faith and conviction. I wanted our movie to be perceived as, primarily, entertainment. I also suggested to Matt that, if we released it now, a portion of the income should be used to help the relief efforts. An immediate response from Paul Crouch confirmed that this was precisely what he intended to do.

After consulting with my publishers, it was decided to postpone this book's appearance, originally intended for early October. Perhaps its bellicose title and cover design should now be changed; maybe there was a final chapter to be added. I began to gradually reconcile myself, though, to the decision to proceed with the release of the film. Although *Megiddo's* theme was apocalyptic, it was not about terrorism but emphasized the eventual triumph of the primal forces of good over those of evil. Moreover, in an uncanny parallel, these very forces of probity and decency were now being rallied worldwide by an energized, scripture-quoting American President—in scenes that could have come directly from the final sequences of our film.

On the evening of September 18th, the prayer meeting was held on TBN. Broadcast internationally by satellite, the service constituted one of the largest ever assembled electronically by the network. In the following days, as mountains of rubble were removed and hope for survivors diminished, the country's mood turned from anguish to anger. Military mobilization began and allies were sounded out. At the same time the uncomfortable realization dawned that the enemy might not be as easily targeted as, say, Stone Alexander's armies at Megiddo. Previously the foes of world peace and stability had flown flags of nationality and bright banners of political allegiance. Now the threat was ubiquitous—in the shadowy shape of borderless, boundless terrorism. And the Beast had yet another name—Osama bin Laden.

A decision was then made to tone down our movie's poster. The more graphically explicit of its apocalyptic elements, such as the aggressive fighter jets and an image of the collapsing Colosseum, were removed. A tag line, "Out of Tribulation Hope Arises," was added and the design of a whole new poster, featuring a post-war idyllic Eden rather than a fiery Armageddon, was initiated.

Megiddo opened nationwide as scheduled on Friday September 21st. Some exhibitors had cancelled it, thinking that its theme might still be unacceptable. Such fears were groundless. The movie tended to sell out from its first midday screenings, with people reported sitting in the aisles and even standing in the doorways. By the end of the weekend the film had proved to be, on the per-screen average of box office income, the most successful in the nation. It more than doubled the receipts of its closest rival. Visits to the web site continued to be equally popular. "Exciting and meaningful, *Megiddo* is the best apocalyptic film yet made" was one response, while another commented on the "powerful performances." I was left with an irresistibly sneaking suspicion that the *Omega Code* phenomenon might just possibly be repeating itself.

There was happy news, too, of the more conventional premiere in Rome, where *Megiddo* had played to a full and enthusiastic house that included many of our Italian production team. I learned, too, that Cinecittá was purchasing land near Bracciano to build another studio, with all the glorious natural scenery around the lake, not to mention my castle, thrown in as an enticing bonus of a back lot.

Over the course of its first week of release, our film maintained momentum to such an extent that, at the weekend, it opened in yet more theaters. Its receipts were still the highest of any movie in major release and bigger than the national average. Despite new competition from some major Hollywood studio films, *Megiddo* still came in at fourth position in the box office league. Perhaps lightning was, after all, striking twice.

On the Friday, September 28th, I flew to Washington on the same airline and type of plane as one that was used to fragment the World Trade Center into a fiery tomb. The flight was not full, and the crew was appreciative of our patronage. Along with the marked upgrade in airport security there was a distinct increase in mutual politeness—perhaps a manifestation of the new and more noticeable unity that now seemed to bind the States. From my usual window seat I wondered how changed was the country unfolding below. Were doors still left unlocked at night and children put in the care of strangers? Were the patriotic stars and stripes that emblazoned the nation after September 11th still defiantly waving? Digging into my breakfast with the new standard-issue plastic cutlery, I imagined that civilian access to the cockpit, such as I had so recently enjoyed, was now a relic of a more innocent and vanished past.

In Washington I again stayed at the British Embassy. Security had been tightened. The underside of my car was checked with a mirror, reviving memories of anti-IRA precautions in mainland Britain. Sir Christopher and the enchanting Lady Meyer were welcoming as ever, despite the constraints on their time occasioned by the crisis. At dinner that evening, Sandy Berger, the National Security Advisor for the Clinton Administration, was a fellow guest. I felt privileged to be present to hear the world situation discussed by actual policy-makers. I was struck by the sheer grueling demands of the work—the endless office hours often extended into the wakeful night with urgent phone calls. I shall never, ever complain again about the excessiveness of film hours. I stayed in an elegant room that is a favorite of Mrs. Thatcher, who has herself been a target of terrorist bombs and who, during the Falklands War, also showed the will to cross the world in order to face up to aggression.

The next evening I hosted the gala opening of a magnificent new performing arts center at the University of Maryland. Scrapping most of my prepared text, I substituted anything I could find that would illustrate the role of the arts in healing and uplifting the spirit. Words spoken by President John Kennedy on another college campus in 1963 were gratefully borrowed: "We must never forget that art is not a form of propaganda, it is a form of truth." However, it was Bernard Shaw's assertion that "without art, the crudeness of reality would make the world unbearable" that struck a particular response. In fact, a reporter from the *Washington Post* requested the quotation for publication in the newspaper the next day. My especial pleasure derived from working with the students onstage and backstage and being energized by the talent and dedication of these young people. They were now in the same position as I was forty years ago, making a commitment to a professional life in the arts. I wondered if their path through the jungle would be as interesting, unpredictable, and rewarding as mine has been? How many pinnacles and pitfalls will they face? Among them were there the pioneers and revolutionaries who will explore new territory and reshape the face of future entertainment?

The post-Armageddon political and military planning continued in the power centers of Washington. As British Ambassador, my host was heavily involved, although his grace under pressure was inexhaustible. We even talked about movies over a relaxing Sunday dinner. He mentioned a favorite scene from *Gladiator* in which the Roman forces are assembled for battle in a dark forest: His mind must have been alive with similar scenarios. It made me appreciate how often movies portray life accurately and meaningfully, and offer escape from the "crudeness of reality" for those whose job it is to manipulate and manage that reality.

I hope that *Megiddo* fulfills its basic job of entertaining. For some it might even change the way in which the human condition is perceived through its appeal to more traditional spiritual values. Hopefully, its theme of moral right routing the forces of evil in this world will soon be enacted in reality. And then—will all the inevitable drama to be fashioned from this bold enterprise be worthy of the event itself? As Cassius enquired after another tyrant's removal in Shakespeare's *Julius Caesar*, "How many ages hence/ Shall this our lofty scene be acted over/ In states unborn and accents yet unknown?" Can even theater fully reflect and encapsulate the intensity and drama of life itself and teach us useful and unchanging truths? I rest my case with a quotation from my own Washington speech: "As an actor, I am convinced that the performer and the performance remain essential to the health and well-being of our complex society. Isolated within the theater proscenium or film frame, humanity can be seen in all its paradoxical attitudes—calling forth both admiration as well as apprehension. But, if our work is properly done, invoking compassion, too. Indeed, 'What a piece of work is a man!'"

October 1st, 2001

ACKNOWLEDGMENTS

Many to thank Jim Bates for his word processing, Adrian Brine for his contribution, Chloe King for her encouragement, and Patt Morrison for her infinitely sensible suggestions.

I would especially like to express my gratitude to Evelyn Chen for her editorial guidance and phenomenal industry, and to Marisa Smith and Julia Hill Gignoux for agreeing respectively to publish and design this book in so short a time.

"Blessed is he that readeth, and they that hear the words of this prophecy." Revelation I, 3

Pat York, Casper Van Diem, Catherine Oxenberg, and Michael York
during filming of *The Omega Code*. Masada, Israel, 1999.

Pat and Michael York during filming of *The Omega Code*. Jerusalem, Israel, 1999.
The Dome of the Rock and The Wailing Wall are in the background.

"Witness your first day in a united world!" Stone Alexander (Michael York) speaking outside the real Colosseum flanked by his wife, Gabriella (Diane Venora), and the Guardian (Udo Kier). Rome, 2000.

Tea break on the set of *Megiddo* in Rome.
Diane Venora (Gabriella) and Michael York (Stone Alexander). Italy, 2000.

On the *Megiddo* set in Rome. From left: Diana Venora (Gabriella),
Rena Andreoli (make-up artist), Michael York (Stone Alexander),
Noah Huntley (adolescent Stone). Italy, 2000.

Michael York (Stone Alexander) and Michael Biehn (Stone's brother David). Note the "youthful" hair. Bracciano, Italy, 2000.

Pat York and Matt Crouch (producer) editing photos during filming of *Megiddo*. Rome, 2000.

Michael York (Stone Alexander) and Udo Kier (the Guardian) working out the "wasp" sequence. Los Angeles, 2000.

© Justin Lubin

The Guardian and Stone Alexander trying to stay cool in the hellish heat. Note the World Zone map behind them. Los Angeles, 2000.

© Justin Lubin

Michael York, Udo Kier, and Michael Biehn on "Stonehenge" at "Mystery Mesa," our California Megiddo. Los Angeles, 2000.

Two commanders in their field. Michael York and Matt Crouch, *Megiddo's* producer. Los Angeles, 2000.

Stone Alexander salutes his massed armies at Megiddo. Los Angeles, 2000.

Stone Alexander in "Africa." Note the long-line suit and the
go-anywhere technicrane camera. Los Angeles, 2000.

Stone Alexander about to hurl Pat's hat at his audience of over a million.
Los Angeles, 2000.

Michael and Pat York, Kennedy Center, Washington, D.C., December, 2000.

Lisa Gerrard and Pat York at Pat's exhibition.
Ghent, Belgium, 2000.